Holy Millionaire

How to Transition From

PROVERTY TO PROSPERITY

To Barry Parker
for loving God
We became family
Thank you,

YVETTE MUNROE

Otherwise indicated all scriptural quotations are taken from the King James Version of the Bible.

Holy Millionaire

Copyright © 2014

Yvette Munroe

Printed in the United States of America

Library of Congress – Catalogued in Publication Data

ISBN 978-1502904683

Published by:

Jabez Books Writers' Agency

(A Division of Clark's Consultant Group)

www.clarksconsultantgroup.com

Jabez Books

1.   Business 2. Personal Finance 3. Christian Living

Dedication

This book is dedicated to my past, and the women who nurtured me: my grandmother, Mary Stewart, who first believed in me, and my mother who always made me feel special. This book is also dedicated to my present: my husband, Courtney, who wants only the best for me, and provides me with a love that strengthens. And to my future; my children -- Courtney Afreya, and Courtney Akiel, who see me as I really am and still think I am exceptional. I honor each of these individuals as they've allowed me to grow and bear much fruit.

I'd also like to dedicate this book to the children of The Institute for the Development of Young Leaders charter school in Durham, NC. They are the object of my current work to provide, promote and prepare a generation to move people from poverty to possibility.

Table of Contents

Preface

A s far back as I can remember, I have always had a burden for helping people, especially when I was a child. My games of "pretend" alway involved me helping others. Usually I pretended to be the teacher when playing school with my childhood friends. Therefore, when I grew up and got saved, and definitely after I was ordained a minister, the burden to help people intensified. But particularly, I had a strong affinity to help those especially in the household of faith. To the members of the household of faith, my prayer is that you, especially you, possess all of the promises of God; for it is your right and your inheritance.

I know sometimes when Christians talk about obtaining monetary inheritance in God, this often upset some, so we get accused of preaching a prosperity gospel. However, I am going to take the risk that you really want to see change in your life *financially*, so I am going to continue on this path.

But just in case you don't read pass this page, there is one thing I want you to know more than anything else. Everything changes if you change your mind. <u>Everything</u>! Our thought life is what controls what we say, what we do, what we see, what we eat, and what we have. If you can change your thoughts, which controls your emotions, then they will produce the change you desire. The Bible says in all your getting get understanding, and in another scripture it says, if you can control your emotions, patience is better than power, and controlling one's temper is **(better)** than capturing a city (Proverbs 4:7; Proverbs 16:32).

This is one of the reasons I wrote this book, so that you might learn how to control and manage your thoughts. In this book, I will expose truths, which are designed to serve you in changing your thinking.

If you are going to be successful in life, the first thing you have to learn to do is manage your thought life, especially when dealing with opposition and challenges. Because every successful person, most likely, viewed limitations and challenges as a part of the process. They did not allow their minds to become captive by setbacks. For them, these crises are viewed as opportunities as well as direction.

As a business developer, I am a consultant to entrepreneurs and those who desire to be entrepreneurs. One of the crucial first steps to working with these individuals is changing their thinking. Your situation can't change until you change. You can make money and still be poor. You can be working towards increasing income and be already wealthy. So when I work with people, I work with them on dismantling their fears and controlling negative thoughts first. If not, these negative thoughts will lead to negative feelings, then to negative self-defeating behaviors including procrastination, speaking against their success and eventually sabotaging their plans either by making poor choices or not making choices or plans at all.

I encourage them to expand their thought life, their vision, and the "container" that holds their dreams, so that they can hold more. You see, money only comes when it is needed. There is a need when a circumstance propels one to action toward a goal, giving purpose and direction to a behavior.

If there is a need, there will be supply. Supply relates to the amount available based on the correct action taken towards resolving the need. In Philippians 4:19, the writer Paul says to the citizens of Philippi who were financing his ministry, *"But my God shall supply all your need according to his riches in glory by Christ Jesus."* Their giving caused all their needs to be supplied. There is a right action that will bring supply to any need.

Many of you are like me when I was living from miracle to miracle with a need just for the basics to be met. During those years, I did not engage much in behavior that was goal directed, nor was I focused and consistent as far as becoming financially independent was concerned. I would ask God to help my check clear at the supermarket to give me enough to feed my children. Guess what? Every day I got just enough to feed my children. Later, I asked for a good parking space at the supermarket. I would ride around the parking lot and pray for a good space. One day as I was doing this, God spoke to me and said, "What if you had faith enough to pray for me to give you the store."

Your vision for your life calls the provision. Money needs a passageway, a reason in which to flow through. What is your vision for your life? If you have a big dream, you are well on your way to accomplishing much. The next step is to become emboldened with the tenacity that comes from single mindedness. The writer, Paul says in Acts, chapter 20, *"But none of these things move me, neither count I my life dear unto myself, so that I might finish my course with joy, and the ministry, which I have received of the Lord Jesus, to testify of the gospel of the grace of God."*

The writer accomplished his mission because of this fierce focus that eliminated the threat of humiliation, any type of circumstance, or even death. His commitment as expressed was given a voice as he took action. Commitment to an ideal must be expressed through focused action; small things done *consistently* to move the project forward.

This is the key to the provision, if we only want money for children and ourselves, it is already being provided for according to that "small" vision. We must increase our vision first, in order to create a need for more supplies. And you have to, like Paul, be ready to say, none of these circumstances move me, and I will continue and finish what I started.

Now, when you begin the journey of success, you need to understand that the natural world and our culture have taught us to rely on our five senses to dictate what we perceive to be true. They teach us to interpret and to operate in the physical (which is the place where limitations exist), but if you ever dare to operate on another frequency in another dimension, you will receive abundance in the spirit, and as a result, you will see it in the natural.

We create our circumstances, therefore, we get what we see and have what we say. Our circumstance is largely a construct of our minds. It's not what we are looking at, but it is what we see that matters. It's time to change how you view your limitations, abilities and opportunities. It's time you changed your world.

At this writing, I have founded four successful businesses, and been involved with the founding of many profitable enterprises: A successful childcare center, a mental health agency, a charter school and a consulting and coaching firm.

It's time we transition from lack into prosperity and from poverty into possibility.

Chapter 1

IS IT WORKING FOR YOU, REALLY?

F or many, work is nothing more than a way to making a living. And if the truth be told, there is not enough wages being earned to live a stress-free or even a debt-free life. Therefore, the faith it takes to even begin to dream of more can be risky as well as paralyzing; when thinking about taking the leap into the seemingly unknown unchartered waters of entrepreneurship. But there is enough information to glean from to encourage you to push beyond your apprehensions. Lots of others did it before you, and you can certainly benefit from their experiences.

It was the latter part of November when I summoned this courage to step out. I delivered a letter of resignation to my supervisor, her bosses and the Human Resources Department. Since 1988, I worked as a social worker in Social Services Departments, first in New York City, then in North Carolina.

I was 10 years old, when my family moved from South America to New York. I was reared in and attended all public schools in Brooklyn. As I think back on things now, I know without a doubt, my fundamental call and purpose is to teach. Because as far back as I can remember, I have always wanted to teach, and it was around the age of 10 that I began teaching younger children in my neighborhood. I would gather them on my stoop and teach them the ABC's and 123's. For me, it was the feeling of being special that I experienced when I gave myself for the advantage of another. I loved that feeling!

These are the signs of your purpose. When you are not sure what your purpose is, think of what you enjoy doing. Because your purpose is often found in what you enjoyed as a child. What was it that made you feel special or alive mostly?

When one door closes it is to expand our view and refine our vision.

Service and compassion have always been my motivators. Wealth and power were not the objects of my passion, they just weren't that important during these years. I remember as a teenager, I would tell people that I was going to be a teacher when I grow up. One day, with a few words, my mother's friend delivered one devastating blow. My mother's friend told me that teachers don't make money. She and others mocked my dreams and discouraged me to do what I had in my spirit to do. I remember a deep sinking feeling. I felt like someone had taken me into the woods and left me to die. Of course I did not recognize it during this time, but my purpose was being undermined. Therefore, I buried the desire to teach.

When one door closes it is to expand our view and refine our vision. The new view is an extension of the old, but it is expanded to accommodate a greater vision. It wasn't long before I was awakened to the fact that I loved to tell stories. I knew this was the case because my family would always interrupt my telling of a tale or experiences with, "Give us the short version." Or they would say, "Your story is too long. You're long winded." I just remember wanting people to get it so badly that I would tell the story in detail.

At this time, I was in the eighth grade and in my English class, we focused on poetry and creative writing. I was an avid reader. I was always hungry for "words." I lived vicariously through the stories in books. Between going to school and doing my daily routine, I couldn't wait to come back to my books. Through books, I would come out of my mundane life and be in Paris in a romance being rescued by an extraordinary man; or be a great lion tamer in the safari of Africa rescuing endangered species. I could be a hero and a damsel in the same week. Books brought freedom and beauty into my life. Through the characters in the books I lived.

As my love for poetry and reading grew some of my teachers in middle and high school saw my affinity for these subjects encouraged me to start writing – to find my voice. One said, "You should be a writer; you tell stories well." This was such an encouragement to me at such a young age. You know, when you are a teenager, you are not clear what you are good at so to have your teacher speak something like this into your life was "gold."

So in college I majored in Journalism. I attended Antioch College in Yellow Springs, OH. I minored in Social Justice.

As I became more and more involved in my education in college, my passion to champion the cause of the disenfranchised and disadvantaged, and vulnerable heightened. I hated seeing people mistreated and I always wanted to give back. I was reading books like *Malcolm X* and *Roots*.

For the most part, I enjoyed college. I felt as though I did a lot of growing up in college, and even though I was not sure what I was going to do after college, I had a knowing within me that I was born to go beyond the status quo. What it was, I did not know, but I was open to see what the world was going to "throw" my way.

After college, I got a job at a local hospital working as a Financial Advisor. I did this for a year and a half, and then I looked for other employment. To be honest, I just could not take it anymore. The environment reminded me so much of one of my sisters who died a few years earlier, which was a very difficult time for my family.

It was in 1989 that my oldest sister, Shannon Lester, was diagnosed with cancer. For two months, she battled this disease. When she was in the hospital, we were there supporting her. This was a very confusing time for us because this was the sister that respected everyone, and I can truly say, she had a real relationship with God.

When she died, my mother especially had a difficult time with it. In fact, she struggled for years coming to terms with her death. We all had our moments, but working in that environment eventually got the best of me: it was too many memories of those awful times. I knew I needed a change. One thing I have learned throughout my life is that if you are willing to move devastation can bring direction.

As I started my job hunt for my next place of employment, I read in the paper that the Child Welfare Agency needed Social Workers. I applied for the job and was hired. So it was in 1989, that I started my career as a Social Worker.

I enjoyed my job immensely, and being a Social Worker provided me the avenue to do what I had always loved – being a community activist and advocate. I got very involved in my hometown civic affairs. I served on the New York City Mayor Commission to help change policies and I served on several boards of for profit and non-profit agencies. I worked long hours, and I worked with the highest standards of integrity through some of the most difficult circumstances. After all, that was how I saw my divorced mother work for 30 years as a registered nurse.

My mother worked two eight hour jobs everyday to support her family. There were seven girls, no boys, in our family, so we were in constant need of much. My father was no longer in the picture, so my mother was the sole breadwinner. I followed in my mother's footsteps and eventually, my hard work paid off, I was promoted to supervisor. Within this same timeframe, I met my husband, Courtney, who was a Social Worker as well. We met at a supervisor training workshop in 1992, and we married in 1993. It was a whirlwind love affair, but I am grateful to God that He gave me the husband I have because he has strong work ethics like me as well. He also loves the Lord and he has a great sense of loyalty and commitment.

During those years, I really loved my job and everything about the type of work I did -- protecting children, removing children from neglect and/or abusive homes, overseeing custody cases, placing children in foster care, counseling and providing supportive services to custodians, and returning children home, but it was emotionally taxing at the same time. So after the birth of my son, in 1997, the time commitment at my job became overwhelming. Therefore, I adjusted my schedule to quiet the growing concern about being gone from home so many hours.

To accommodate my desire to spend more time with my young son, I changed my hours at work and started working nights as an on-call child protective services worker, however, I was unable to find adequate childcare for the few hours I needed in the early mornings when my husband had to be at work and I had to be in the office staffing and handing over cases. After several attempts and changes in daycare providers, I was at my wit's end with little options.

> *If you are willing, you can learn from your family history and break the patterns of behavior that replays the past in the present giving you the same result generation after generation.*

I talked with some of our neighbors, and they, too, were having problems with daycare. Not knowing exactly how to resolve this daycare challenge was a difficult time for me, but I knew we had to do something different. The tipping point was when my mother had a stroke on the job and suddenly was unable to work. She had worked as a registered nurse for 30 years, and was replaced as "quick as a wink," suddenly unable to do the very thing she had done for 16 hours every day for 30 years.

If you are willing, you can learn from your family history and break the patterns of behavior that replays the past in the present giving you the same result generation after generation.

A mini awakening occurred after what I saw her job do to her. I began to do some soul searching. I began to assess my situation. Her ordeal set off an alarm within me about what I was doing; where I was headed. I was set for the long hard hours like my mother, but then I realized if something happened to me, I would be greeted with a replacement worker unceremoniously, without hesitation.

Looking back over my life now, I realize God is always calling us, we just have to listen. You see, my husband and I had two beautiful and intelligent children. I had earned the respect of employers, colleagues, neighbors, and family members alike. I reached a place that all of my mental prowess, my smarts, and my rational mind could take me. I was connected, admired, loved, and doing meaningful work. My children were in ballet and Gymboree. We went to the Farmer's Market, took walks, met other middle class mommies for play dates, went to museums, visited with grandparents and did all the things associated with the American dream.

We also had a nice new house that we built in a nice new middle class neighborhood. My marriage was more than I dreamed, the hero came out of the books of my childhood, but he was better than the dream. However, I went to bed at night and cried.

Everything I thought I wanted, I went after and got, but I was crying myself to sleep. I couldn't explain it. After I read my children bedtime stories, kissed them goodnight, tucked them into their own beds in their own beautifully decorated rooms, I would go into my room with my handsome (loving, caring, responsive husband), and after he fell asleep holding me tight in his arms, I would cry. Silently, I would feel like I was lost in the woods with no light and no path. The season of transition was a familiar territory, but it was no less devastating.

As I was at my wit's end, at the end of myself, it was at this time that I was told by my twin sister that she and her husband were starting a church. Out of loyalty for them and a desire to support them, I began to attend services with them. It was over the next several years that I was introduced to the real person of Jesus, an all-powerful, all-loving God, an active Holy Spirit and a faith producing Word.

I believed the Word, so I said it. I believed it, so I expected it. I believed it, so I shouted it. I believed it, so I cried out. I believed it so much that I put a demand on it to perform, and the Word performed. Eventually, I found my life no longer lacking in purpose. My path was clear and I knew I wanted more out of life than what I was experiencing. I wanted to make sure the hours that I was giving (working on a job) were important as well as defined by me, so with little discussion, and great astonishment of others, I resigned from my "stable" government job and decided to open a home daycare.

This was in 1994, and trust me; I didn't fully know all that I know today, but God was positioning me for where I am now as an author, serial entrepreneur, motivational speaker, consultant, and owner of a multi-million dollar producing company. God will always fulfill His Word.

By 1999, I began attending Bible study and church services regularly at my twin sister's church in Durham, NC. My pastor (my sister's husband) would teach about the love of God and how He was full of compassion, mercy and kindness. He taught us how God was an abundant God, who loved us to the extreme and showed it by paying the ultimate, incomprehensible price for us, the life of His Son for mine.

This was not the first time I heard the gospel in my life, because I initially got saved at the age of 16. However, hearing the gospel preached during this time in my life was like hearing it preached for the first time. There was something about it that was different. This time I heard that there were no conditions on God's love, and that He loved me even when I didn't know Him. That He was faithful to me even when I was not faithful. This time I was taught that the creator does not hold back His love waiting for us to be perfect because He was the only perfect One. I was told that there was no condemnation in Christ and that anyone who received Jesus no longer had to perform, but just receive. I was made to know that God paid the price that I may go "scot-free."

Empowered by this understanding, my relationship with God deepened and I received His grace, love and mercy. I no longer hesitated to go to Him and cry out boldly for help. My thought life began to change, my mind was being renewed, and I was hungry for the Word of God. I "ate it" as often as there was a free moment. I responded by surrendering my time, plans, will, business, and money to God. It was not out of an obligation, but out of a deep understanding of His great love towards me, and His desires for me. As I applied my understanding of His love for me, I only wanted what He wanted.

As my mind changed, my sight, energy, strength, and vision for life changed and my capacity to contain the abundance He had given to all who are in Christ increased.

As my mind changed, my sight, energy, strength, and vision for life changed and my capacity to contain the abundance He had given to all who are in Christ increased.

When I started the daycare, I started out caring for two kids. As I grew spiritually and my mind expanded with the Word of God, I began to notice, my business began to prosper more. However, at first, it did not look like this. In fact, my income went down significantly, and I made about 19,000 dollars the first year. However, prior to this, I was only making $38,000 annually.

At this time, I was thinking and feeling like a failure financially even though there was an unexplainable peace within. To the natural man, not only was the "job" not working, but also the new "business" wasn't working either. But I continued to read my Bible everyday and learned all I could about God's will for us to prosper. I was so hungry for the Word of God that I allowed myself to be tutored by a myriad of teachers and preachers in church, on television and on the radio. I inundated my mind and my home with the Word of God.

Greatness is a part of our Abrahamic blessing and we are not only called, but also positioned to reign in this life.

To my amazement, my student enrollment grew from two children to four children to eight children, so forth and so on. Eventually, we had to find a location to house the daycare. We had outgrown our home. For about three or four months, we looked for property where we could relocate the daycare. After diligent searching, we thank God; my husband did find a facility that we could possibly buy for the daycare. When we checked into it, it was in our price range and we secured it for our daycare.

We had the daycare for five years, and running it was truly a learning experience for me as a new business owner. God used this experience to teach me many stewardship and business strategies, but one thing I knew, I had tapped into something with God. And if I stayed close to Him and believe His Word, I knew I was going to come out on top.

Yes, the years we were open, we had many up and downs. Often, we were challenged with operational procedures, but no matter what we encountered, we assessed the situation and continued going forward.

Greatness is a part of our Abrahamic blessing and we are not only called, but also positioned to reign in this life. When it was time for God to transition me into my next level of elevation, I felt impressed in my spirit to close the daycare. By this time, I was making $80,000 a year, and I wasn't sure of everything He was doing, but I knew He was with me, and if I would continue to seek Him, He would guide my steps. *The steps of a righteous man are ordered by the Lord* according to the Word of God. So it was in 1999, we decided to close the daycare.

In preparation for closing the daycare, I met with our staff and parents and I let everyone know that in 30 days, we were shutting down the daycare. As you can expect, parents were disappointed and saddened to see us close. My husband had quite a bit of resistant to this decision as well. Much of his concern was financial and wanting to take care of his family, so of course, I understood it, but I knew I was still doing the right thing by my life.

There was NO MORE grace! That which started out being joyous and pleasant was no longer there. Running the daycare from day to day began to be difficult for me. While I certainly wanted to be successful financially, but this was not my primary goal when I started the daycare. Again, I wanted to help people. As the daycare grew, more and more operational tasks consumed my thoughts and days, which was not what I wanted to do eight hours a day. To be honest, I really felt that my season was up with the daycare, and this particular purpose had ran its course and it was time for me to move on.

SETTING THE STAGE

In the beginning God created us in His image and likeness and declared that we were created good according to the Book of Genesis, Chapter One. He then blessed us by saying, *"be fruitful and multiply; replenish the earth, subdue it and have dominion over every living thing that moves on the earth."* The Bible also tells us that after Adam "fell" in the Garden of Eden in Genesis, the consequence for his sin was that the whole world fell. This sin introduced sickness, pain, death, hard work, poverty, and loss of dominion. However, God provided a plan to redeem us from the curse to re-establish our rightful place with Him. Using a man named Abraham, God made a promise that He would bless all nations of the earth and that Abraham's seed would be blessed. In Romans 9:6-7, the Bible says, *"It is not as though God's word had failed. For not all who are descended from Israel are Israel. Nor because they are his descendants are they all*

Abraham's children. On the contrary, it is through Isaac that your offspring will be reckoned."

In other words, it is not the children by physical descent who are God's children, but it is the children of the promise who are regarded as Abraham's offspring. I was being taught this and I embraced this truth, so I knew no matter what our circumstances were saying or showing us, we had a covenant promise that we were to be blessed.

The Bible also says in Galatians 3 that Jesus became a curse for us that freed us from the curse. Poverty and lack are a curse. We are redeemed from the curse of the law. Why was this done, so that the blessing of Abraham would come on us through Jesus Christ by faith? It says that we are children of God through our faith in Jesus Christ and that Christ is Abraham's seed. As well, if we believe in Christ, we are in Christ and therefore Abraham's seed, and heirs according to the promise. I believed this and I stood on this.

Chapter 2

From Heir to Holy Millionaire

He who hungers and thirsts after righteousness, the Bible says shall be filled. I read the Bible all the time, believed what it said and constantly sought His presence. As I was being taught in this newfound teaching, I heard about how I was an heir of the Father and a joint-heir with Jesus. Boy was I excited when I heard this, because my pastor and other Bible teachers I was listening to began to explain what this really meant. They began to explain what an heir is and what an heir inherits.

During these years, I could feel my faith growing in insurmountable ways to believe God to do the impossible. It was in 2007 that my business first grossed over a million dollars. But before I share this process, first I want to make sure we are on the same page. I want to share with you what I learned about being an heir and a joint-heir. This information is so important to the process of shifting your mindset in order for you to receive your blessing, so I want to make sure you know the information that solidified my hope and desire that God would do something great through me.

Often people are quick to start striving for things that they do not have the foundation or basics for, so in the short term, it looks like they have succeeded, but in the long term they wind up defeated. To avoid this mistake I want you to know everything that pushed me into achieving all that I have now. Let's begin the journey!

WHAT IS AN HEIR?

If you want to do great things for God, you need to understand your position in Him. When you are born again into the Kingdom of God, you become an heir of all that the Father has (Galatians3:29). Then the obvious question should be what does the Father have? According to the book of Psalm the 50th chapter, every creature is His. He owns the cattle on a thousand hills. He owns the world and everything in it. In the book of Haggai in the 2nd chapter and 8th verse, God says the gold and silver are mine. Whatever the Father owns is yours as well. Why, because you are an heir.

What is an heir? Heir is a legal term identifying a person who is entitled to the benefits or property of the predecessor (the person who came before or who held the position before). An heir is the rightful person to inherit the endowment or quality of the one that gives it. Therefore, an heir is a person who is entitled by law or by terms of a will to inherit the estate of another.

Being found in Christ, we are heirs of God. Therefore, we are given the same inheritance as Christ as co-heirs. When we receive the gift of eternal life through receiving Jesus Christ as Lord and Savior, we receive salvation and are redeemed from the curse.

And the word," inheritance" is the act of passing on property, titles, deeds, debts, and obligations upon the death of an individual.

WE ARE JOINT-HEIRS WITH JESUS

When I learned I was an heir to the Father, I also learned another incredible truth; I was joint-heir with Jesus. A joint heir is someone who is entitled to the benefits at the same degree as the other who they are joined. A joint-heir is a co-heir; a partner or fellow participant in the same inheritance.

Being found in Christ, we are heirs of God. Therefore, we are given the same inheritance as Christ as co-heirs. When we receive the gift of eternal life through receiving Jesus Christ as Lord and Savior, we receive salvation -- declaring with your mouth that Jesus is Lord and believing with your heart that God raised Him from the dead (Romans 10:9-10); and are redeemed from the curse.

Believing puts you in right relationship with God. Romans 8:14 says, *"For as many as are led by the Spirit of God, these are sons of God."* You receive

Christ as Lord, then you are an heir of God. Galatians 3:27 says that we are all sons through faith in Jesus Christ.

In order to restore us and give us back the glory, power, favor and access to God, He gave the promises and blessings to a man who believed God. We know him as Abraham, the father of our faith because he first believed God and God responded with promising him *and his descendants* to bless them. His descendants became known as the Hebrews because they were wanderers (later known as Israelites) because God changed their ancestor Jacob's name to Israel (Genesis 32:28). Now these physical descendants were heirs to the promise and all others were outsiders or strangers to the promise. But through Jesus, God reconciled all who would believe in Jesus as the Son of God into one blessed, empowered, unstoppable people who are heirs to the promise.

Ephesians 2:14-18

> *"For he himself is our peace, who has made the two groups one and has destroyed the barrier, the dividing wall of hostility, by*

setting aside in his flesh the law with its commands and regulations. His purpose was to create in himself one new humanity out of the two, thus making peace, and in one body to reconcile both of them to God through the cross, by which he put to death their hostility. He came and preached peace to you who were far away and peace to those who were near. For through him we both have access to the Father by one Spirit.

Now because of Jesus, we are no longer foreigners outside of God's favor and promises to bless. Because of our faith alone in the finished work of Jesus, we have access to God's grace. Making us now heirs to the promise of which we are legally entitled. In Christ Jesus we are Abraham's seed.

In Galatians 3:5-9 we read,
"I ask you again, does God give you the Holy Spirit and work miracles among you because you obey the law? Of course not! It is because you believe the message you heard about Christ. In the

*same way, "Abraham believed God, and God counted him as righteous because of his faith. The real children of Abraham, then, are those who put their faith in God. What's more, the Scriptures looked forward to this time when God would declare the Gentiles to be righteous because of their faith. God proclaimed this good news to Abraham long ago when he said, "All nations will be blessed through you. So **all who put their faith in Christ share the same blessing Abraham received** because of his faith." (NLT)*

Now, this was accomplished according to Galatians 3:13 by Christ rescuing us from the curse pronounced by the law. When Jesus was hung on the cross, He took upon Himself the curse for our wrongdoings. The NIV says in Galatians 3:26-29:

"You are all sons of God through faith in Christ Jesus, for all of you who were baptized into Christ have clothed

yourselves with Christ. There is neither Jew nor Greek, slave nor free, male nor female, for you are all one in Christ Jesus. If you belong to Christ, then you are Abraham's seed, and heirs according to the promise.

The Message Bible says, *"...since you are in Christ's family, then you are Abraham's famous descendants, heirs according to the covenant promises."*

Now before Christ came and before we received Him, we were condemned to live as slaves to the law and slaves of sin. We were not able to access God or lay hold of His promises. We had no authority and had to accept whatever lot we were given. The Bible refers to that in Galatians this way:

"So also, when we were children, we were in slavery under the basic principles of the world. But when the time had fully come, God sent his Son, born of a woman, born under law, to redeem those under law, that we might

receive the full rights of sons. Because you are sons, God sent the Spirit of his Son into our hearts, the Spirit who calls out, "Abba, Father." So you are no longer a slave, but a son; and since you are a son, God has made you also an heir. Now you, brothers, like Isaac, are children of promise."

So now, we are righteous before God (in right standing with God), justified and given the promise as Abraham's seed. Every promise of God is received by grace through **NOW** faith.

As we look to the Lord with gratitude for such love demonstrated in His grace towards us, we know we are not without help; we are not without power. As believers, we have the right and the power to take authority over any situation and command it to change. We don't have to beg God, we can go boldly to the throne of grace and obtain favor and help in times of trouble. We can ask and know that nothing good will be withheld from us. It is our covenant right.

As heirs it is our right to be free, to be the top, to be victorious.

We have the blessing back, therefore, we should be fruitful, increasing, replenishing and subduing the earth.

HEIRS OF WHAT?

The Bible says we are more than conquerors through Jesus Christ (Romans 8:37); we are overcomers (1 John 5:4). It says that we are the righteousness of God through Jesus Christ (1 Corinthians 5:21), and that we can do all things through Christ that strengthens us (Philippians 4:13).

The heritage of the children of God is that no weapon formed against them shall prosper (Isaiah 54:17). These and many more promises are made available to believers as children of God. But I don't want you to miss this essential part; we are joint-heirs with Jesus. All promises I just mentioned above and many others are our inheritance that were made available to us when Christ died on the cross. However, an heir not only gets the title, deeds, estate, and property, but He also gets the debts and obligations. But the good thing here is that Jesus had no debt and He fulfilled all our obligations of the law. He took care of everything, therefore, freeing us from the judgment that was made against us.

The debt was paid in full and overflowed to all who received to be debt-free. So we are free from the curse, condemnation, sin, shame, and from every evil thing that plagued us. We are placed back in the garden with dominion and authority restored.

We have the blessing back, therefore, we should be fruitful, increasing, replenishing and subduing the earth.

We have the favor of God, which gives us an advantage -- a supernatural empowerment to prosper. We have peace with God which means God is for us and not against us. We have been given inherited grace -- a power that makes us unstoppable. God says in Psalm 2, *"I am your father and you are my son ask of me and I'll make the nations your inheritance, and the end of the earth your possession."*

TRANSITIONING

When God began to push me into my next level of success and to close the daycare, this was a very difficult time for my family. We had bought property based on my current income ($80,000/yr) and closing the daycare would throw the family into a financial crisis. Even though I knew this, deep down inside of me, I knew I was still doing the right thing.

To transition from the daycare business, I immediately felt led to start looking for a job as a social worker. I looked for openings in several places in my region, and within the first 30 days, I found an opening at a mental health agency in a neighboring city online. As I shared with people about this opportunity who knew about this agency, I was told that this agency did not hire minorities. Regardless, I was still led to apply. I applied for the job and I was offered the position as a social worker for mental health services. I had never worked in the mental health side of being a social worker, so a lot of the things I was learning were new. However, I was eager to learn, so this was not a problem.

Just as quick as I got the job, we, the staff, was informed that this agency was going to be closing in seven months. The State of North Carolina was making some structural changes to how they were providing services to clients. They were divesting from the provision of direct services. They were moving to privatization of community based mental healthcare. By doing this in the long run, it would save them money and effort.

One day as I was pondering on the situation, I thought to myself, why can't I apply to the State to become a private provider? This thought began to resound in my spirit repeatedly. Then I began talking to co-workers about this idea. Nobody wanted to take this risk including my husband, who had been a social worker for many years. Some even told me if you open up your agency, we would work for you.

After much pondering and deliberation, I decided to apply for my state license to become a private provider. The application process, needless to say, was very tedious and long. I had to prepare all kinds of documents and an operational manual. To this day, I don't know how I did it except for the grace of God.

Completing the application process took six months. God supernaturally ordained two people to assist me through this process. These two people would come to my home almost every night from 7pm to about 1 or 2am to assist me with this process. From September 2005 to January 2006, we worked on the Operational Manual. Once we completed it and sent it in to the State of North Carolina, it took one month before we heard back from them. It was on February 3, 2006, that I received notification that the state had approved us to be one of their private providers.

The former location we used for the daycare was used initially to be our office building for our agency, but in three months, we had to expand. We had 25 staff members and 100 clients. In one and a half years, we had 200 clients and 70 employees – comprised of licensed social workers, professional counselors, case managers, medical doctors, psychologists, a Human Resources Manager, and a host of other contract and office personnel.

We were extremely excited about what the Lord was doing for us as well as working hard to keep up. By April, my husband quit his job, and joined me in running the business. Initially, he came aboard as a social worker, but after about three months, he saw the need to fill the position as CFO, which was wonderful because my husband actually went to college for this. My twin sister, June, also joined the Agency. She was hired to be the Program supervisor because of her extensive experience in social work.

Before I opened up the Agency, I did have some inkling how this could affect my personal finances, but I did not know to what extent. In a matter of a year and a half, I was overseeing and managing millions of dollars.

Before I opened up the Agency, I did have some inkling how this could affect my personal finances, but I did not know to what extent. In a matter of a year and a half, I was overseeing and managing millions of dollars. We were able to buy an even more beautiful home in an incredible neighborhood, buy better cars, and send our children to the private schools of our choosing. But the thing that really "drilled" it home for me is the day my bankers called and asked to meet with me. They said they wanted to talk with me about my finances. I agreed and we set the day.

The day came for us to meet and the bankers arrived at my office around noon. What they shared with me, I had never heard. They explained to me how the bank only insured a certain amount of money and that the amount of money I had in their bank had to be managed differently - talking about a "fish out of water." So they assigned me a Financial Advisor, then I met with my attorney and began doing estate planning. All of this was completely foreign to me. However, I was up to the task. I listened, read up on everything and learned from my past. The ironic thing is that I had more control over my money when I was making $19,000 than the millions. Now, I am not complaining, it is just a different world when you are managing a company that is grossing multi-millions of dollars. It has been eight years (2006-2014) that our Agency has opened and we can truly say the Lord has been faithful.

We are able to pray for clients with their permission. For more than 5 years, we offered a weekly Bible study for all who wanted to attend at the office. On our office walls we have our vision statement and our declaration of our faith. We know it was the Lord that gave us power to get wealth. My husband and I are thankful every day.

Chapter 3

THOSE THAT GOT SHALL GET

O nce my understanding and beliefs were right, it set me on a course that could not be detoured. The flight plans for my life changed. Abundance (or anything else) is received in the Spirit first and the Spirit brings it into being (in the natural).

Abundance comes to abundance. Those who are full will have full*ness*. That is what God spoke to me from Genesis, chapter 15. Fear not for I am with you. I am your shield, I am your great reward, and I became satisfied, content, and full. That word, spoken first to Abraham, and then deposited into me (my spirit) gave me fullness; an abiding, comforting, empowering understanding that I had the ultimate wealth. God, the creator Himself was the reward. My wealth had nothing to do with anything physical. The God of all was with me and I was His. I was complete and full to overflowing. He told me because I was His, He was not only with me, but He was within me and I in Him. If I let go, He would do what He wanted to do with me and His will was always for my "great" good.

He gave Himself to me through Jesus Christ. He reconciled me to Him, and He, working through Jesus Christ, returned me to His grace and favor. His plan was to get me back in good standing through allowing Jesus to suffer and die as punishment for my sins. I now had peace with God through Jesus Christ. I was right with God and now had access to the throne of God so that I could get unlimited favor to meet every need.

The Bible says that those who receive God's abundant provision of grace and the gift of righteousness will reign in life through Jesus Christ. This is so important. Without receiving His abundant provision of power to meet every need and defeat every foe and seeing ourselves as blameless, justified; thus entitled to His empowerment and help, then we cannot reign in this life as kings. For a king must know that he has all power and authority and that he is in his rightful position.

Wealth is more than money. It is fullness to the overflow until you can feed others off of you.

My definition of wealth is having all sufficiency (competence) in all things that I may always have enough (as much as necessary) for all things and to give to charitable donations. Sufficient means no lack. If you had sufficiency to eat, you have enough to meet the need. The lack or need is met with plenty.

Wealth is more than money. It is fullness to the overflow until you can feed others off of you. In my practice, I often remark about a colleague, "she has a wealth of information," or "he has a wealth of experiences." Wealth is neither good nor bad. It is an amount. It is so much that it causes you to be full of it to the point of others being able to use what you have.

Now prosperity, on the other hand, does take on a positive meaning, but prosperity is also more than money. Prosperity covers and includes every area -- spiritual (relationship with God through receiving Jesus Christ as Lord and Savior by believing in your heart that God raised Jesus from the dead and confessing with your mouth that Jesus is Lord); physical (good health); psychological (wellness in your mind, stable in your emotions, thinking and feeling, and an alignment of your will with God's will); vocational (profession or career); relational (devotion in marriage, obedient children, healthy friendships, honoring of parents); and financial (economic plenty in an amount that you can take care of your needs and the need of others).

The paradox that many Christians live with and accept is that you can't be prosperous in every area. This is not true, to prosper is to grow and advance along the way until you get to the desired or blessed end. People accept that they have to sacrifice something to be successful or that no one is prosperous in everything. They accept that you can be prosperous or successful in your physical health, but be unsuccessful at business. You can be successful or prosperous in business and experience a failed marriage or have an unsuccessful relationship.

However, Apostle John prays in 3 John, verse 1 that we above all should be prosperous and be in good health, even as their soul prospers. He identifies prosperity as a desirable thing for the believer. With this being said, I was inspired to define prosperity in this way: Prosperity means to successfully grow and advance towards the desired end.

WALKING IN IT

In Proverbs 4, the Bible says in all your getting, get understanding. It also says wisdom is the principal thing. It tells the reader that wisdom will keep, defend, and protect you. Wisdom will promote you, bring you honor, place grace on your head, and give you power to be delivered. The way of wisdom is walking in the truth -- doing what is right. Wisdom will allow you to tolerate the uncertainties of life. With wisdom, there is an increased awareness and assurance of how things play out over time. It gives an enlarged capacity. It produces a space, and makes room for the ways, purposes and power of God to be revealed.

Understanding and wisdom are two different things. Understanding is discernment, comprehension, or proper interpretation of how something relates to a particular. It's a certain perspective usually gained through knowledge. Understanding applied is wisdom. The Bible says let your heart retain my words. Keep and act on my words and live. If you know better and do better, you are wise, and wisdom will promote you. But not all of us do the "better" that we know.

The man who walks in the truth, applies the word/understanding goes on a road that will lead to prosperity.

To actually change your mind and apply new behavior to old situations is wisdom. Wisdom is the application of understanding.

In 3 John 1:2-4 it reads: *"Beloved, I pray that you may prosper in all things and be in health, just as your soul prospers. For I rejoiced greatly when brethren came and testified of the truth that is in you, just as you walk in the truth. I have no greater joy than to hear that my children walk in truth."*

It is possible that you can know the truth and not walk in it. The Apostle John was pleased with the news that Gaius was walking in the truth. The implication is that walking in the truth is not automatic when you know the truth. When the Apostle reveals his prayer, we see him praying for the prosperity of the recipient of the letter as he was walking in truth. Because of this, his soul was prospering.

Walking in truth takes you on a journey to prosperity in every area. The Greek word for prosperity is *euhodos.* The proper translation is a good road. On a journey a good road will have a plain, smooth path, you will make progress and advance, and if there are any hindrances, there will be help greater than the hindrance to nullify and make the hindrance of no effect.

On a good road, you will reach the destination. In Psalm 1, the Bible reveals this truth, *"Blessed is the man Who walks not in the counsel of the ungodly, Nor stands in the path of sinners, Nor sits in the seat of the scornful; But his delight is in the law of the Lord, And in His law he meditates day and night. He shall be like a tree. Planted by the rivers of water, That brings forth its fruit in its season; Whose leaf also shall not wither; And whatever he does shall prosper."*

The man who walks in the truth, applies the word/understanding goes on a road that will lead to prosperity. The expected end for that man is prosperity. We are all on the journey called life, but some of us take the road of prosperity. The picture of this man is not that he doesn't experience seasons. Obvious in the text is that the tree experiences seasons and that some season may cause leaves to whither. But this man's leaves will withstand harsh seasons and his leaves will not wither. And in the right time, after the hard time, he will produce an outgrowth of prosperity. He prospers in whatever the season he is in as well as produces things useful to feed others.

An example of this man is found in the story of Joseph:

Genesis 39: *"Now Joseph had been taken down to Egypt. Potiphar, an Egyptian, who was one of Pharaoh's officials, the captain of the guard, bought him from the Ishmaelites who had taken him there. The Lord was with Joseph so that he prospered, and he lived in the house of his Egyptian master. When his master saw that the Lord was with him and that the Lord gave him success in everything he did, Joseph found favor in his eyes and became his attendant. Potiphar put him in charge of his household and he entrusted to his care everything he owned. From the time he put him in charge of his household and of all that he owned, the Lord* **blessed** *the household of the Egyptian because of Joseph. The* **blessing** *of the Lord was on everything Potiphar had, both in the house and in the field. So Potiphar left everything he had in Joseph's care; with Joseph in charge, he did not concern himself with anything except the food he ate"* (NIV).

We see Joseph in an unenviable position. He is a slave. Betrayed by his kin and sold to foreigners. He was bought by an Egyptian captain to work as a slave in a menial role, but when Potiphar realized that he did his tasks with ease and was successful in all his assignments, he promoted him to his assistant and eventually turned everything, all of his affairs over to him knowing that all of it would prosper under Joseph's attention.

Joseph knew God. He saw God work on behalf of his father and grandfather. He understood that God acts on behalf of those who trust Him. Joseph was shaken, but not stirred. He not only knew God would deliver him, but he acted on that understanding. He didn't ask Potiphar for an easier assignment nor did he sleep with Potiphar's wife to obtain promotion. He just did his job to the best of his ability and kept believing and hoping in God. Later, Joseph is thrown in jail after being falsely accused, but he still trusted God and understood God would not forsake him.

The story continues in verses 20-23.

"Joseph's master took him and put him in prison, the place where the king's prisoners were confined. But while Joseph was there in the prison, the Lord was with him; he showed him kindness and granted him favor in the eyes of the prison warden. So the warden put Joseph in charge of all those held in the prison, and he was made responsible for all that was done there. The warden paid no attention to anything under Joseph's care, because the Lord was with Joseph and gave him success in whatever he did.

Do you think Joseph was complaining or receiving everything with thanksgiving or meeting every challenge with an "I can do it attitude." I think so because the Bible said Joseph continued to be blessed. It doesn't matter the external position or circumstance, you can prosper when you are in it because the road will eventually lead you being successful coming out of it and into a new season of prosperity where you will feed others. The Bible tells us that those who walk in the way will be prosperous. Their children will be mighty in the land; the generation of the upright will be blessed. Wealth and riches are in their houses, and their righteousness endures forever. Even in darkness light dawns for the upright; for those who are gracious and compassionate (Psalm 112:2-5).

In case the reason for prosperity is still unclear to you, let me end this section with this. Prosperity is the blessing of God. It is the advancement, the growth and the progress of God's people on the earth to take them to a place of peace and security as well as allow them to "feed" others off of their *tree*.

Prosperity is the demonstrated power of God in your life; the ability to meet the needs of others. Prosperity is being equipped and empowered by God to be successful in every area of your life. Prosperity's purpose is not to achieve great health, acquire great goods and sit around doing nothing. No, it is for us to use to do good and bless the earth.

2 Corinthians 9:8 says, *"God is able to make all grace, every favor and earthly blessing, come to you in abundance, so that you may always and under all*

circumstances and whatever the need, be self-sufficient—possessing enough to require no aid or support and furnished in abundance for every good work and charitable donation."

That's the Bible, *every earthly blessing...in abundance... for good work.....*Satan has already lost. His only hope is to defeat God's people in this life so that it could look like God didn't win and prevent more people from trusting God.

> *"For I know the thoughts that I think toward you, says the Lord, thoughts of peace and not of evil, to give you a future and a hope"* (Jeremiah 29:11).

Ephesians 1 says God has blessed us with all spiritual blessing in heavenly realms. If indeed we are blessed with all spiritual blessing, empowerment or allowance, then we are able to appropriate or take anything in the physical realm according to the will and purpose of God.

Yvette Munroe

Chapter 4

WALKING IN THE POWER

THAT'S WITHIN

Scriptures reveal that the glory and power of God is with the people of God -- *I give you power to step on serpents and scorpions* (Luke 10:19). We see in 2 Corinthians that we have precious riches in us, *"We hold these treasures in*

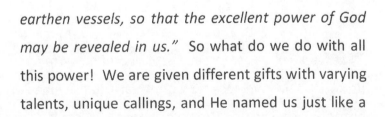

If we are not

experiencing *this*

power, it is because we

believe our experiences,

which are filtered

through our emotions

rather than the Word of

God.

earthen vessels, so that the excellent power of God may be revealed in us." So what do we do with all this power! We are given different gifts with varying talents, unique callings, and He named us just like a father names His children. He called us to walk in love, promote the gospel, bring hope into hopelessness, and forgive those who offend us. He called us the head, the first, the church, His body, and He called us blessed. God called us kings and priests, children of God set apart.

If we are not experiencing this power, it is because we believe our experiences, which are filtered through our emotions rather than the Word of God. We believe what we did will qualify us or what we didn't do will disqualify us. We believe what people say about us rather than the Word of God or we believe our addictions rather than the Word of God or our own reasoning over the Word.

People said you would never be anything, but God says you are a royal priesthood and a chosen person. They say you will fail, but God says nothing will harm you. They left you, but God says you are never left alone. They say you will not make it, but God says I give angels charge over your life. God says I know the plans I have for you and they are good.

If we believe the Word of God, if we get a revelation of His Word concerning us, then all the vain things we pursue will fall off. They say they don't love you, but God says you are the apple of His eye. I wrote your name on the palm of my hands and I numbered every hair on your head.

We have help. We have the power of heaven. We have the love of God. We are never alone. We are not forsaken, abandoned or neglected. If our parents let us down, God will lift us up. He takes pleasure in our prosperity -- physically, financially and relationally. He is a God who heals us and provides for us.

The God of abundance, the God who creates something out of nothing, has given us His love, His power, and the right to succeed. It is God's will that every need in our life be supplied. He is faithful to His Word. He says in His Word, He will be with us always. His Word is true and He stands ready to perform it. He says seek Me, you will find Me. He says if you walk and live in My Word, the Word that says you are victorious, triumphant, more than a conqueror and an overcomer, you will access the power that is in you.

When the Word lives within you, you can ask for whatever you want, and it shall be given unto you. You have to walk in His Word. I promise you, it is more powerful, helpful, and it is more wonderful than any other word, feeling or experience. God loves us and His plan is that we prosper. As well, He has given us His love, which is unstoppable, unending, and it is power to overcome the trials of this world and to fulfill the call of God on our lives. In 1 Corinthians 12:7, Paul says the manifestation of the Spirit is given to everyone to profit. In 1 Corinthians 6:19, it says that our body is the temple of the Holy Spirit who is in you.

Acts 17:24 says it this way, in Him we live and move and have our being. In 2 Corinthians 6:16, God says, I dwell in them and walk with them, and I will be their God. The same God that is above all, in all, and through all, lives in you. Galatians 4:6-7 says, God sent the Spirit of His Son into your heart, so we are no longer a slave, but a son. God, who commanded light out of darkness has shined in our hearts to give us the knowledge of His Glory (power), which was displayed in the face of Jesus Christ according to 2 Corinthians, verse 4. Now, in Ephesians 3:20, we are reminded that God is able to do exceeding abundantly more than we can ask or think, according to the power at work within us. This alone is incredible. No matter what we think or ask for, it is still something bigger to think and ask for. 1 John 4:4 says it this way, greater is He that is in you than He that is in the world.

Now, let's look at Revelations 21:3. It says, God's dwelling place is now among the people. 1 Corinthians 6:17 records it this way, he who is joined to the Lord becomes one spirit with Him. You have the power to overcome every odd that has been stacked against you. God said His people could pass through the sea of trouble and He would subdue it. He would strengthen them and they will live securely. The power of God resides in us for us to do greater works in Him, therefore, we must choose to believe Christ above all of our experiences, feelings, plans.

Don't Quit –Ephesians 2:1-10 & 22

God is building you into a temple fit for His dwelling. He says the struggle is over; the guilty verdict is overturned and the power to prosper is with you. Wherever you go, whatever the situation that leaves you bound and without an escape, remember God is with you and in you, and no power is enough to hold you back from living above.

The story of Paul and Silas is recorded in the book of Acts in the 16th chapter. Paul and Silas found themselves in a most difficult place especially for believers. They were wrongfully accused, attacked, and beaten, counted amongst the criminals and placed in the darkest recesses of the prison. Not only were they imprisoned, but accused. Their livelihood, reputation, ministry, and health were under attack. They were bound and seemingly without opportunity of escape. But they were with much opportunity for advancing the kingdom and preaching the gospel. And what seemed like failure was an opening to demonstrate the power of God and save many.

Perhaps they were praying for ministry opportunities, for doors to open, for a ready audience. Maybe they were praying for souls to know Jesus. Perhaps they prayed for the power of God to fall. Maybe it was the jailer that was praying for relief, for help, for truth, or peace. Whatever the reason, the men of God found themselves in an unenviable predicament. It would have been powerful enough that Paul and Silas prayed and sang hymns while locked up and bound, which would have been a great witness to the other prisoners. But that was not enough for God. God released the chains and unlocked the prison doors. Paul and Silas still stayed in the prison because in their spirit and soul they were never bound. They didn't have to run out, they had already walked out. They weren't excited when the circumstance changed because they had already received it and that was why they worshipped God liked they did. They believed God in the face of their adversity knowing that He was going to deliver them.

Their release occurred before others saw it. Their faith caused the door to open, and their actions caused them to gain credibility, influence and favor. They experienced success even while they were in prison and the Kingdom of God advanced. Let's look at this story beginning in verse 22.

22 The crowd joined in the attack against Paul and Silas, and the magistrates ordered them to be stripped and beaten with rods.

23 After they had been severely flogged, they were thrown into prison, and the jailer was commanded to guard them carefully.

24 When he received these orders, he put them in the inner cell and fastened their feet in the stocks.

25 About midnight Paul and Silas were praying and singing hymns to God, and the other prisoners were listening to them.

26 Suddenly there was such a violent earthquake that the foundations of the prison were shaken. At once all the prison doors flew open, and everyone's chains came loose.

27 The jailer woke up, and when he saw the prison doors open, he drew his sword and was about to kill himself because he thought the prisoners had escaped.

28 But Paul shouted, "Don't harm yourself!

We are all here!"

29 The jailer called for lights, rushed in and fell trembling before Paul and Silas.

30 He then brought them out and asked, "Sirs, what must I do to be saved?"

31 They replied, "Believe in the Lord Jesus, and you will be saved—you and your household."

32 Then they spoke the word of the Lord to him and to all the others in his house.

33 At that hour of the night the jailer took them and washed their wounds; then immediately he and all his household were baptized.

34 The jailer brought them into his house and set a meal before them; he was filled with joy because he had come to believe in God—he and his whole household.

The Christian who is able to abound in praise, thanksgiving, and expectation when in adverse situations, will receive in the physical what they already have received in the Spirit.

You might have heard about a person having a poverty mentality, which simply means that the state of poverty is on the inside of a person. I can give you an abundance of money, but you would still do the things that poor people do including extravagant consumerism without investing or producing, and soon you may find yourself without again.

The flip side is also operational. You can live with very little and behave like there is abundance. The Christian who is able to abound in praise, thanksgiving, and expectation when in adverse situations, will receive in the physical what they already have received in the Spirit. We have to see our loving God as seated on the throne and Jesus sitting at His right hand interceding for us along with the Holy Spirit empowering us. If God is for us, who can be against us? He who did not spare his own Son, but gave Him up for us all, how will He not also, along with Him, graciously give us all things? (Romans 8:32 NIV)

My Scripture for living: I have been crucified with Christ and I no longer live, but Christ lives in me.

The life I now live in the body, I live by faith of the Son of God, who loved me and gave Himself for me (Galatians 2:20).

My perspective or revelation about my life is that I've given my life to Jesus in exchange for His life, His resources, and His right standing with God. I've given to Him my life (for He gave His life for me), and that includes my time, resources, talents, energy, desires, and plans. My life or decisions are not for me, but for Him. I am the manager of the life I live. I manage my time, relationships, money, and opportunities as well as being conscious of the fact that Jesus is bringing those things to me for my tending and caring. It is His and when I can do well with little, I can be trusted with more. All my resources, time, money, talents, and relationships serve the purpose of God.

Chapter 5

SUCCESS PRINCIPLES

f you fail to plan, you plan to fail. I am a big believer in principles and plans. I plan my year, my month, my week, and my day in advance. I am never bound by my plans, but with a plan, I have some frame in which to begin, and a guide in the middle of my journey and a tool to use in assessing my progress. Here I offer you the keys to my success. If you can plan your life using some of these principles, I believe that you can find success. They are universal and will work for anyone.

1. **You are not your thoughts, but your thoughts produce who you are**.

   What you think is not who you are. Who you are is what you think. In other words, you allow a picture to be held in your mind, then you live in it, and then you live it out. I am not my children, but my children are the product of my spouse and myself. Our DNA, genes created them. They look like us, have some of the same strengths and challenges, have similar mannerisms, personalities and preferences. Same with our thoughts. They come from the germination and cross-pollination of our intellect, experience and exposure.

They are not us,

Your thoughts are the key factor to increasing your income, cash flow, favor and the goodness you see.

but they are produced by us. Mainly, our thoughts come out of a practiced perception or way of interpreting neutral events. A favorite example is that my thought is based on a fact that my mother and father divorced and my father was not available to me for most of my life. Now, while this was truly part of my life experience, I have to give meaning to it before the thought can be active. I ate every meal, felt very loved, and I lived in a safe environment. No bad thing came to me as a result, but I can use cultural interpretations of what that meant. I can assign meaning to it. Either I can be depressed that my father was not there or I can be overjoyed that the things that came against me did not hinder me. Our thoughts come based on exposure, then we assign it an emotional value, which inevitably we will see our world through its window.

Your thoughts are the key factor to increasing your income, cash flow, favor and the goodness you see. Unless there is a mind shift, a paradigm shift, there will be no external change. As you see yourself in your mind this is what you will do. I know it's popular to say, "If we know better, we do better." As much as this is a clever sounding statement, it is untrue. Massive amounts of information is available to us through the information highway -- the internet, yet, people still don't eat better, live better, love better, and do better, so just having information available is not the solution. Knowing is about being acquainted with an experience or the acquiring of information or intelligence. Until the mind is renewed, the change can't happen. Knowing is not enough. Until we change our affection, our attachment, our source of truth, our understanding (which is the use of information to interpret facts), we can't change our circumstance.

Our mind holds information and memory. That memory is not only knowledge about facts, but emotional intelligence is stored there as well. Information that contains strong feelings based on the feelings that were powerful in the experience in which you acquired the knowledge is what will be exhibited. For example, my daughter loves drinking tea. It reminds her about her times growing up when she and I would have tea together. She felt happy, safe and warm. On the other hand, my son hates tea. It reminds him of a time growing up where he felt like I was unavailable. We hold an emotional memory that is more powerful than any other, which eventually we will exalt as truth. We hold it dear. It has become our source and we value it as our safe haven responding to it as it urges us to.

To change our minds, we must set our affections on God and esteem and exalt His Word. In God's Word, it says, He is with us, and that He gives us an abundance of grace to meet every need. We either believe this or we believe our circumstance, which is being filtered through our emotional thoughts. If we look at our circumstance and think we don't have, we won't have. *Them that's got shall get.* If you lack, you lack. If you are sad, you are sad. If you are sick, you are sick. But the opposite is true. If you are healed, you are healed. If you are prosperous, you are prosperous. You might ask, "How can I be something I'm not?" Through the Word of God and with the help of others who have mastered it.

Confession to change your thoughts:
I am full because God promises that He will not withhold any good thing from me. I have everything I need to meet this moment or the creator would not allow it to confront me. I am in Christ and He is in me. All power is given to me to execute the will of God on the earth. God has given me power to tread upon serpents and scorpions and nothing will harm me.

Is this happy talk? No, it is believing in the Lord Jesus Christ talk. It is resting in the Word of God talk. It is valuing what God says about you over what your situation says. It's seeing the opportunity and open door in all situations through the knowledge of what you possess in you. Remember, the same power that raised Christ from the dead is in you.

EXPOSURE

The way to think better is to expose yourself to what you want to think about. Whatever we like/don't like, and all of our preferences: how we do things, what we find important, or who we are comfortable with was all taught to us without our knowledge, consent or willing participation. The cultures of our homes, neighborhoods, cities, countries, and groups that we identify with taught us what to think.

If you grew up in a home where there was a strong, loving father, you will like, seek or value a strong loving husband. If you grew up with ambitious people or people who value accomplishments, you will seek to achieve. If your surroundings emphasized looks, you become aware of fashion and how things look. I remember my mother saying, "Clothes make a man." All of our exposure and experiences have formed and informed our thinking. It has formed it to such an extent that we believe it to be our thoughts, or I've always been like this, or this is just the way I am. The grumpy person says, this is just the way I am in the morning, but that is not who this person really is. This is the thought he has accepted.

Our thoughts are not our own. They are what we receive because of our exposure and experience. The mind in its attempt to understand our experience(s) will store it, catalogue it, and form a library of emotions to be used in situations to inform our response to similar experiences. A poem that expresses this well hung in my childhood home and reads this way:

Children Learn What They Live

If children live with criticism, they learn to condemn. If children live with hostility, they learn to fight. If children live with fear, they learn to be apprehensive. If children live with pity, they learn to feel sorry for themselves. If children live with ridicule, they learn to feel shy.

If children live with jealousy, they learn to feel envy. If children live with shame, they learn to feel guilty. If children live with encouragement, they learn confidence. If children live with tolerance, they learn patience. If children live with praise, they learn appreciation. If children live with acceptance, they learn to love. If children live with approval, they learn to like themselves. If children live with recognition; they learn it is good to have a goal. If children live with sharing, they learn generosity. If children live with honesty, they learn truthfulness. If children live with fairness, they learn justice. If children live with kindness and consideration, they learn respect. If children live with security, they learn to have faith in themselves and in those about them. If children live with friendliness; they learn the world is a nice place in which to live.

As the mind changes the interpretation of your experience, your mind offers you new thoughts to help you understand what you are experiencing instead of saying I can't do that, you say I can do all things through Christ who strengthens me.

Whatever you have been exposed to makes you think what you think. If you've seen people lose money by investing in something or another and you saw/heard how devastating that was for them, you may think that investing is not a good idea. But your brain just received partial information and stores it into what may be useful. However, if upon further investigation, you noticed that that the investment product was foolish and ill advised, and what if the person invested in a snake oil salesman's product, then your thinking can become informed and you may hold another thought that says, if you invest foolishly, you will lose your money. Therefore, you may be inclined to investigate before investing.

Thoughts are not yours. Your mind forms them from the pictures that it receives from physical experiences. If you change the source of the information and change your exposure, new pictures will form, and inadvertently, new thoughts will come.

The Bible says labor to rest in His Word. Translation: Work to believe the Word. Translation: - Give yourself over to the exposure of the Word of God. In the early days of me transforming my life, I only watched the preached Word on TV (and HGTV a bit). I only listened to Gospel/Christian music. I only read for pleasure Christian books. I only spent time with faith people. I overdosed on it until it became my experience. I exposed myself to an atmosphere of words that taught my mind new realities. New information was introduced to my mind, and my mind was challenged to find a place for that information and to make it useful.

As the mind changes, the interpretation of your experience, your mind offers you new thoughts to help you understand what you are experiencing instead of saying, I can't do that, you say I can do all things through Christ who strengthens me.

Instead of seeing yourself defeated, you say I am an overcomer: I am more than a conqueror through Christ. As you continue to do this, your mind will show you a picture of Christ on the cross exchanging His righteousness for yours. And by this act on the cross, you see Him giving you an inheritance with the saints and causing you to be empowered in every aspect of your life.

The Bible says as a man thinks so is he. Henry Ford put it this way, *"If you think you can do a thing or think you can't do a thing, you're right."*

We must expose ourselves to people who are doing and accomplishing what we want to do or hope to accomplish. We must capture your thoughts and hold them prisoner to hope. Only allow your thoughts to think of the successful, desired results of your dreams. You **absolutely** must control every thought, measuring it against what you desire. If it is **NOT** your desired result, flip the script, turn the page, and shut it down.

Just keep doing what you are doing because eventually, your thoughts of good will take over.

The mind has to have thoughts, but if you don't allow it to have evil ones; it will only have good ones. It is the only ones allowed. Deliberately, intentionally, meet with people who are loving and kind, who are encouragers and motivators. As well, think on and about people that are inspiring and energetic. If you don't know people like this, find them on the web, on TV, in a book or a magazine. Reach out to them or live through them vicariously. Find stories of redemption, or rags to riches. Bask in stories of great love and where dreams were realized. Fill your thought self with your own dream and mix it with the dream results of others until you are so full of your dream and their results that they are one, then you will be unstoppable.

2. You have to see it before you see it

Rest in the idea that you are unstoppable. That your expectations will be fulfilled. When you rest in this truth, you will work to achieve the dream. My daughter once said, "Rest doesn't produce rest, work produces rest."

In order to rest, you have to work. The required work is to believe in the Lord Jesus Christ and His finished work. When you receive what Christ did on the cross as perfect and finished, then you will find rest from your work. Why? Because you will now work from a place of rest. It is not that you don't work, but now the work is sweatless, stressless, prosperous, even though people might think you are driven or a workaholic, but actually you are resting in Christ (a supernatural empowerment that makes what should be difficult easy).

I remember the long, difficult hours of being a daycare provider. As a sole proprietor, the hours were long, the income did not match the emotional expense, and it was an intense labor. I knew this in my head. However, it was very easy for me physically and emotionally. I had a grace and an empowerment that caused the work to flow easily and I was fully satisfied and grateful for all my work. People would sometimes acknowledge my experience by saying, "I don't know how you do it." Or "I couldn't do this." Or "I wouldn't do that." All I could think was this is so easy.

Looking back, I now get it. They were right in the natural. It was an impossible position to feel so free, satisfied, empowered and blessed all at the same time. But it was not natural. I had placed my life in God's hands and labored to rest. I also fought to believe God's Words and intentions towards me, so I fixed my eyes on His crazy, boundless love demonstrated by His Son. I saw that He was using me, that He had delivered me, and that He was **"making"** my way. I knew that my life in His hands would become powerful, effective and purposeful. I knew the answers were provided, every need was met, and that every step, He was with me and He was taking care of me. There was no worry or fear. There was only a vision of greatness and my good.

3. WINNING BY LOVING

This is actually more difficult for me to teach than almost anything else because I've always had a deep love and abiding compassion for people as far back as I remember. I see people as I see myself. The more people act out or seem lost or are struggling with issues of life is the more tender my heart feels toward them. They, I imagine, are hurting and alone, and they are afraid even more than the rest of us. Or they don't have the skills to get help or are void of the voice that protects and gives. They are left only to take. My heart goes out to them. I don't tolerate or condone bad behavior, but it does speak volume about the level of despair and loss they are experiencing who engage in these unseemly behaviors.

I love all people. I love the ways we are different and the ways we are alike. I love the unexplainable intricate unique ways we show up around the world. Every person fascinates me. I know we all bring something valuable to the world and when we show up in any situation, we have the power to heal or be healed, and in fact that is why we showed up. I think about what makes them tick, what drives them, how did they show up now and why did they like this? I value every person as much as myself. It is my most valued asset.

I recognize the God-good in every individual. For God created all of us and there is an innate proclivity within all to seek our creator. It is the hole that was made in our souls when man fell from grace and lost the glory of God (read the book of Genesis). Loving someone isn't an acceptance of what they do; it's a realization of who they are as the greatest creation of God. It is the knowledge that we all need God and none of us are perfect.

Low self-esteem will cause a person to not be able to believe God as well as not receive His grace to its fullest. At the same time, if we consider ourselves more highly than others, we will miss seeing the value of God's work in all created things. If God made a mistake with a person or there is no value in them, then God could make a mistake in our situation, therefore, there could be times where our situation is of no value. But that's not true with God because all things are possible. God did not think anyone wasn't worth saving. He came for everyone. When God made man and declared that man was good, even though it seemed hidden and that it cannot be found, there is still a declaration of God's Word over lives. He Himself called us good. I find good in people easily. I am able to consider their choices from their point of view.

I experience the good in others with ease. Even when I feel disappointed, betrayed, despised, misused, or abused, I am always seeking to understand my role, their drivers, and how it can be minimized, or prevented in the future. I look at these infractions more as an uncovering of a truth that has always been there, and this uncovering as a vehicle of change. When they were hurtful, the hurtful thoughts or intentions were always there, I just didn't know it. Therefore, I received it as a lesson, and an opportunity to improve and grow.

I inherently believe that everyone deserves love and I try to extend that to all. To teach it, I first go back to the Word of God that says that faith works by love (Galatians 6). If you are to make your faith operational, you must love. Well, how do I love? By believing the truth that whatever happened or happens cannot stop God's love for you or your ability to be successful.

Most of the time when we are jealous, angry, unkind, or unloving, it is because we are afraid. Afraid that someone is better. Afraid that someone will stop us. Afraid that someone can steal our dream, affect our destiny. Afraid that there is not enough for everybody. These are all lies that the devil introduced to our natural systems to cause us to act outside of love. When we act outside of love, we act outside of God's providence, and we come out of the hiding place. We expose ourselves to external elements and circumstances, and consequences of acting without the protection of God. For God's love surrounds us as a shield. When our faith is working through love, we believe that God is with us and for us and will not withhold any good thing from us. This is the secret place in which faith is operating. This is the place of no fear for love drives fear out. Fear can't live where there is faith.

In that place of faith, you believe God is your refuge and fortress and there is nothing no one can do bad to you that can come against the power of God in you and on you and for you. In that place, you hate no one because there is no fear. Where there is no fear, there is only love. Acting from that place of love operationalizes faith, while taking what love gives.

As tough as it is for me to teach, I know there are many who experience difficulty in feeling love for some people. Especially if they have gone through a difficult time. I can only tell you what I know. I know for sure if you abandon your feelings and just love anyway, your feelings will comeback.

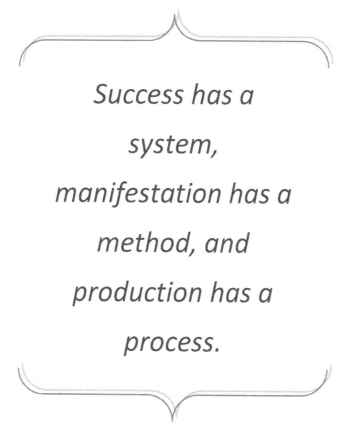

Success has a system, manifestation has a method, and production has a process.

Love is an action word. Love is not a feeling. It's a verb meaning to show kindness, compassion, and loyalty. The Bible uses all action words in defining love in 1 Corinthians 13:4-7. It says love is and love does. It says love keeps and love rejoices. When you say you don't love someone no matter what's the reason, the truth of the matter is that you are saying, *I don't act correctly towards others.* When you don't act correctly toward others, you are sowing negative seeds in the earth. However, there is a remedy, and it is available and simple. Ask God to forgive you and to help you to do right even in the face of wrong even when you don't FEEL right, and God will do it. Consider and meditate on God's great love and desires for you, then begin to act in loving ways towards others, and I guaranteed before long, you will FEEL love.

Love is felt when love is done. People are drawn by love. People are healed by love. People are changed by love. People are delivered by love. People are set free by love. And people are empowered by love. Your loving ways will be the foundation of your winning ways.

BE INTENTIONAL

I often say success has a system, manifestation has a method, and production has a process. What I mean by this in the simplest form is that all people who are successful (consistently getting the desired result of their actions) are intentional. They, whether they know it or not, are engaged in a system or process that results in success.

A system is a set of connected parts forming a desired outcome. For instance, the Bible says, and we know that all things work together for good; and many of us stop reading the verse right there because its sounds good. However, the scripture continues by saying it is for them that love God, to them who are called according to His purpose. It is a set of seemingly unrelated parts: Love God, then the calling to His purpose forms all things working for good to them.

Let me be clear, there are many (infinite in number) instances where God acts miraculously and supernaturally suspending the laws of nature and systems to act providentially and theoretically, but we do have free will and live in a natural world and can use the revelations of scripture to inform our behavior and in doing so unlock a system that had been inaccessible in times past. This passage of scripture in context is speaking of believers suffering and their confidence that the sufferings will result in good for them who love God and are seeking/executing His purpose. Now, remember earlier, I mentioned that love was an action word. The writer says this is to them that love God (meaning have set their affections on God, to those who esteem God above all else, to those who acknowledges God as supreme).

The call is for all believers. The purpose is to be fruitful, multiply and replenish the earth as well as subdue it taking dominion over all living things that move on the earth. It is reiterated in the great commission in Matthew 28, "Go ye therefore into all the world..." and bless the earth. This is a great example of a system, take note that each part has to work together to produce an outcome.

The system of success is a set of parts when engaged together will always work to produce the same result. The system of success is intentional whether or not the participant is conscious of it or not. Using the system, you can predict the results.

A key component of success is a clearly articulated vision. The common use of articulate is spoken words. I'd like to use it here to mean expressed both in speech and in written form. There are two sets of adjectives used in this passage to describe vision. I have met countless people who tell me they have a vision, but when we get right down to it many of them have not yet clarified their vision. Usually people say, "I want to own...or do such and such." They are steeped in the activity, but they rarely can tell you why, and when they do it. Often what they do, does not line up with their lives as articulated through their behaviors controlled by misguided principles.

A clear vision makes it easy to see what the end will be. It will be easy to be understood by others, readily able to be taken advantage of and held without effort. A clear vision tells everyone what is important. It is value driven. A clear vision is location focused. It tells everyone where you are and where you want to be. It is result-oriented. It says what will be produced and who will benefit. A good vision statement identifies the primary goal/purpose of the activity, therefore, making it easy for steps or strategies to be employed along a path that leads in a fixed direction.

When vision is expressed clearly, it shows others how to be, which way to go, and what they will see when we get there. It generates activity. When the vision is in thought form, it can't generate specific,

When vision is expressed clearly, it shows others how to be, which way to go, and what they will see when they get there.

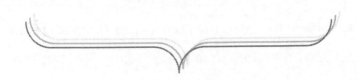

meaningful activity of others focused on accomplishing it. When vision is spoken and declared, it transforms from nothing into life from spirit into the physical. When it is written, it goes through a clearer process because it can be seen and handled by others. It can be repeated more exactly, and it can be further developed and refined.

A written vision is the reason why we are taking this trip. This will tell us which map to use, what direction to go, and what will happen when we get there. The banking, lending, and business industry knows this quite well that's why they all ask for a business plan. Although these two are very different documents, it is their way of looking at your vision. Written vision is necessary. That's how I read it in Habakkuk, chapter 2, ***"Write the vision and make it plain that he may run who reads it."***

A clearly articulated vision comes from a source. That source is usually at the center of our thinking and frames our perspective. In Proverbs 3:1-2 and in Psalm 1:2-3, the scripture says, if you meditate on the Word of God both day and night and keep God's Word in your heart, your way will be prosperous and successful. What you have in your heart, what you've been thinking on and meditating on becomes the frame for the picture or image you've developed about your life's work. If you've been looking at business leaders or millionaires, or TV personalities, or celebrities, your vision for your life comes from them. If you have meditated and fed on the Word of God, your vision comes from Him, therefore, your success is undeniable, because He knows the way to your expected end.

MANIFESTATION HAS A METHOD

The Latin meaning for manifestation is to make public or to appear —"He that keeps my commandment I will love him and manifest myself to him."

The commandment is to love: Love God, love yourself, and love others. You have to love and believe in yourself, your dream and your talents. When your dream is bigger than your ability, be it internal, external or otherwise, then you have a God-given dream. That dream comes from God and only God can accomplish it. When we stand in our position of righteousness and in the light of God's great love for us, we see the power and favor we have with God, so our accomplishment are in direct proportion to our revelation of this truth. If we are not worthy, we will do worthless things. If we are deeply loved, we usually perform according to the expectations and giftings given to those who are deeply loved. In other words, we have to get a revelation or see a truth even if it's hidden prior to us possessing it. In other words, He loved us so and was determined that we would have the best, as well as be the best that He subjected Himself that we might be released from failure and lack.

To see the manifestation, you must increase your love of yourself and your confidence in God's love and commitment to your best. You must hold a positive, high regard for yourself and see yourself as God sees you. You are His handiwork created in Christ to do good works. Expect that He has you right where you need to be. Expect that He who began a good work in you will complete it. Expect that your future is brighter than your past. Expect that God is not finished blessing you. Expect to see God's goodness in the land of the living. Expect a harvest because He loves you.

When we participate in activities contrary to our beliefs and hopes, when we are only hearers of the word and not doers, therefore, we produce outcomes that are undesirable.

THE PROCESS OF PRODUCTION

According to Hebrews 11, faith comes by hearing and hearing by the Word of God. Also Romans 5 tells us that our justification that was produced by our faith in Jesus has caused us to have peace or harmony with God. And while we glory or praise God for access into this grace, we should also praise Him or glory in tribulation knowing that tribulation or trouble produces perseverance or determination. And this is the determination character or the strength to do what is consistent with your values, principles and positive outcomes (hope or expectation). Always remember, expectation brings about a manifestation.

Production for this writing is referred to as the power packed twins: faith and patience. You see if you are employing a system, if you are filling your heart with the knowledge of Jesus' love for you and extending that great love He has for you to others, and if you are vigilantly managing your thought life, then you will be in a process that will undoubtedly produce. Truth is; we are producing all the time whether or not we know it, and it is realized through our activities. We are constantly enabling things to materialize or come to be.

If we speak failure, lack, or fear, we get what we say. If we think on certain things that are not good, sooner or later it will come out of our mouths. The Bible says out of the abundance of the heart, the mouth speaks. When we participate in activities contrary to our beliefs and hopes, when we are only hearers of the Word and not doers, therefore, we produce outcomes that are undesirable. And when we chose to participate in these activities, we then operate from a deficit standpoint. The Bible says in Ecclesiastes 9, that time and chance happens to everyone. It is up to us to seize the moment. The way we seize the moment and produce the desired result is to come into agreement with the desired result. We must have agreement in our thinking, acting and saying. This is not about doing right; it is first and foremost about believing right.

Meditate on the love of God and expose yourself to the preached Word until you find yourself full of the thoughts, words and deeds of Jesus. Many people believe and don't know that they have to come into agreement with what God's

Word says about the situation. If the word says ask and you shall receive, then when you ask, confess that you have received it and go believing. If you believe there would be evidence, then it will come to pass. I direct my car on a certain road everyday because I believe I will get home if I keep on moving forward. Let the believers believe. If you believed, you would be living it. I'm not calling you to act on it, I'm asking you to believe. Believing will cause activity. Faith is the confidence that what we hope for will be seen. It is a certainty that what we do not yet see already exists. The psalmist said "I would've fainted unless I believed (trusted was fully assured) that I would see the goodness of God in the land of the living."

Faith gives reality or existence to a thing that is not yet seen with the eye. Faith is our sixth sense. It sees it, confirms it, and acts on it. Our faith exerts pressure or a demand on the unseen to show itself. Faith is the subsistence or **life** of things hoped for; the evidence or demonstration of things not seen. So if I receive deliverance from poverty through faith in God, then this is belief in demonstration of my faith in God that He is a rewarder of them that

Holy Millionaire

diligently seek Him. Faith comes by hearing and hearing by the Word of God. Poverty does not develop faith because faith **ONLY** comes by hearing the Word of God.

Trouble produces determination or perseverance as previously discussed, but it does not produce faith. Faith can be strengthened in an experience, but it only comes by hearing the Word of God. Our faith can produce perseverance, but perseverance does not produce faith. Because when faith is proven it produces endurance, steadfastness and patience. Now that we have a working definition for our discussion of faith as giving life to a thing, let's look at its twin, patience. Patience is right on its heels because faith calls forth patience.

"We don't want you to become lazy, but to imitate those who through faith and patience inherit what has been promised." Hebrews 6:12

For we hope for that we see not, then do we with patience wait for it." Romans 8:25

"Knowing this that the trying of your faith works patience and let patience have her perfect work, that you might be perfect and entire wanting nothing. James 1:3

Faith without patience is like a farmer who plants a seed and comes back the next day and digs it up because he saw no fruit. Once your faith is activated and you expect God to deliver on His promise, then all you need to do is wait with expectation and it will come to pass. In James 5:7, the Bible says be patient unto the coming of the Lord. It says look at the farmer who waits for the precious fruit of the earth and has long patience for it until he receives the early and latter rain. If we wait for the Lord to come into all of our situations, and have faith, He will come with justice and reward. I recall the parable of the sower in Luke chapter 8. Jesus says to the crowd a sower sowed some seeds. Some fell at the wayside, some fell on a rock, some fell among thorns, but some fell on good ground and sprang up and bore fruit. Jesus explaining the parable said the seed is the Word of God. Those planted at the wayside, on a rock, and among thorns represent people who hear the Word and the Word does not bear fruit in them, but He said the seeds planted in good ground represent they which in an honest and good heart having heard the Word kept it and brought forth fruit with patience. We must receive the Word regarding our finances, hold the Word in our hearts, as born again believers in the Lord Jesus Christ, then we will bring forth fruit in time.

Faith works with patience to drive out lack and usher in maturity or ripeness. When a fruit is ripe, it is at its best to nourish and sustain others. If faith is the seed that when planted grows and develops in our womb, then patience indicates when faith is mature like a midwife speaks of timing and positions us to deliver.

Excellence is a habit, not an achievement. The success of anything is dependent on the consistent daily, moment-by-moment actions taken. Success is what people notice as your daily actions (sacrifice or offering for success).

Fish Mouth Blessing Matthew 17:27

When you confess the Word, meditate on the Word, obey the Word, and stay with the Word, the Word will direct you into plain paths. It will be an ease. The anointing to access the blessing and the plan of God will be fully upon you. What seems foolish now becomes the obvious answer and the impossible becomes possible. You will have abundance more than enough to do all that God has called you to do and supply every demand.

For years now, I have been meditating on the scriptures that says owe no man nothing, but love, so now I am confessing, I am debt-free. Extremely scary stuff considering I own expensive homes, luxury cars, and commercial properties. However, the expectation of freedom from debt came from God through His Word. A borrower, it says is a slave to the lender. So I have been meditating and confessing debt freedom. In the midst of my engaging my faith in this way, my daughter who is a college student some distance from home asked her father and I to buy her a house, so that she can live off campus. After considering the benefits of owning real estate and recognizing that the economics of the time has presented opportunity for real estate acquisition below costs, and that my daughter's plan to have roommates that would offset the mortgage made for good investment, so we agreed to the proposition.

But prior to this transaction, my husband and I had experienced numerous property purchases without any difficulty. However, this transaction for no apparent reason would not go through easily. Although we were approved, because of our resources, the banker kept being prevented from doing the paperwork for the loan. Every Friday for more than a month the loan closing was scheduled, but at the last moment was not processed or ready. Our agents and closing attorney were involved with pressing the bank to fulfill the commitment. This situation got to the point that the seller was threatening not to wait any longer. During this ordeal my daughter had to live in a hotel. But without explanation, the paperwork was not ready week after week. We were approved, but the papers just weren't ready at each closing date. I continuously prayed for the loan process to be successful, while daily confessing debt freedom. One day I felt the Holy Spirit in me began to shrink back as I confessed debt freedom. I found no power in my confession. The Spirit spoke to me and said your confession of debt freedom has blocked the loan processing department from completing the paperwork. This is when I realized that I had grown my spirit in this area and I could not acquire any more debt in contradiction to what I was believing for and what I was calling to happen. As I was commanding financial freedom and debt cancellation, I was engaging in a transaction that was opposite my confession and my declaration was blocking the new debt. My confession was stronger than my resource, which was easily able to incur new debt. My confession was stronger than my lack. You see, if we declare a thing and walk in agreement with the declaration, then we will see it materialize.

Something has to win. You can't confess you are the righteousness of God and do unrighteous things and believe that both can operate at the same time forever. You will still be the righteousness of God, but your words won't have power. You can't confess God will supply all your needs according to His riches in glory and not tithe. There is a spiritual and natural transaction that is in play as you call those things you are believing to happen. Because eventually your faith-filled words will create a new reality. It's only a failure if you quit. When you continue, it's a part of a success story. Never give up!

We have to call those things that are not as though they were. We have to command our condition to be restored to access the riches in the spirit and bring it into the physical. The Word of God is spirit and it is life.

SPEAKING AGAINST ANOTHER PERSON

The Bible says in Malachi 3:16-18, *"Then those who feared the Lord talked with each other and the Lord listened and heard and a book of remembrance was written concerning those who feared the Lord and honored His name. On the day when I act says the Lord they will be my treasured possession. I will spare them just as a father has compassion and spares His son who serves him. And you will again see the distinction between the righteous and the wicked, between those who serve God and those who do not."*

> *You can't confess you are the righteousness of God and do unrighteous things and believe that both can operate at the same time forever.*

Often people speak against wealthy preachers or pastors, against wealthy people in general or even against wealth itself. This speech is toxic and anti-productive to wealth acquisition. You are telling wealth that you despise and reject it. Be careful not to spend any time being negative, instead be patient and long suffering and speak well of others. Remember, the words in the Bible in the book of James, Chapter 3:9-10, which says, we praise God and with the same tongue we curse man who is made in the same likeness of God, and out of the same mouth comes blessing and cursing this should not be so. Speak blessings and not curses. Curses in this context is not referring to foul language rather negative speech.

Now, I want to share with you some faith-full words to say instead of fear-filled words. When your spirit hears you say this and your heart understand these changes, things will become supernaturally available to you. Those words will focus your vision on what God has done and will do. Just like God set Abram to envision his future by looking at the stars. ***Abram's expectation, words and actions changed as he looked up toward heaven.*** Our situation will change as well, if we will continue to look up and not down. If we will continue to look into the perfect law of liberty our situation will forever shift in His presence.

Chapter 6

DAILY CONFESSION OF FAITH FOR FINANCIAL INCREASE

- My God will supply all of my needs according to His riches in glory.
- The cattle on a 1000 hills belong to God and I am His child.
- God will not withhold any good thing from me.
- All things work together for my good because I love the Lord.
- God is for me not against me.
- God is my shield and my exceeding great reward.
- The Lord is my shepherd, I shall not want.
- I am more than a conqueror.
- God is my helper.
- Wealth and riches are in my house.
- God is enlarging my territory.
- My God is my recompense.
- God owns the silver and the gold.
- God blesses me daily.
- God has blessed me with all spiritual blessings.
- I am God's child.

- Good measure, pressed down, shaken together and running over blessings are men pouring into my life.
- I am blessed going and coming.
- God has given me exceedingly abundantly more than I can think or ask. Whatsoever I asked believing in Jesus's name is given unto me.
- God is not a man that he shall lie nor the Son of man to change His mind; He said He would bless me and I receive His blessing.
- God has given me everything I need for life and godliness.
- I am an heir of God and joint-heir with Christ.
- I am the righteousness of God through Christ Jesus.
- I am Abraham's seed and am entitled to the promise God made to Abraham to bless (empower him to produce) and God is my only source.
- God is with me.
- God is showing me favor and opening doors.
- My Heavenly Father knows what I have need of and is supplying my need with abundant

provision and all grace is abounding toward me.

- Victory is mine.
- In the end I win.
- I am the head and not the tail.
- God has empowered me to prosper.
- Though a 1000 may fall at my side and 10,000 at my right hand, it will not come near me.
- I am enlarging my tent.
- God has blessed me indeed and enlarged my territory.
- God has placed me in a wealthy place.
- God is using me to bless the world.
- God is giving me strategies and wisdom, knowledge and discernment that I may act excellently at all time.
- I reign in life through Jesus Christ.
- No weapon formed against me shall prosper. I am blessed to a thousand generations.
- Abundance flows into my life, people love to pay me.
- God is loading me up every day with great provision and supply.
- I am debt free.

- I sow bountifully, so I reap bountifully.
- I have the wealth of the wicked and owe no man anything, but love.
- The blessing of the Lord has made me rich and adds no sorrow.
- Jesus became poor that I may be rich.
- The blessing of the Lord has come upon me and has overtaken me.
- God has commanded the blessing on me and has increased my finances.
- All the work of my hands prospers.
- God has given me plenty of goods.
- God has established and strengthened me, and I am equipped with all grace and have all sufficiency to meet every need with abundant supply, which enable me to give charitable donations.
- Christ has redeemed me from the curse of the law.
- Jesus has delivered me from poverty and given me wealth.
- God is able to make all grace (every favor and earthly blessing) come to me in abundance, so that I may always and under all

circumstances and whatever the need, be self-sufficient—possessing enough to require no aid or support and furnished in abundance for every good work and charitable donation. I will be enriched in all things and in every way, so that I can be generous, [and my generosity as it is] administered...will bring forth thanksgiving to God.

- I have given and it is given to me good measure, pressed down, shaken together, running over.
- Men give to me all the time.
- I do not lack any good thing, for my God supplies all of my need according to His riches in glory by Christ Jesus.

BLESSING AT WORK (references from Leviticus 26, Deuteronomy 8, Numbers 24, and Proverbs 10)

The blessing is the anointing to inherit or possess the best or the wealth of the land you are in; the land in which you are an outsider. Psalm 3:8

says, the Lord's blessing is upon His people. We, who are in Christ, are His people. We are in the family of God. We have been adopted, grafted into the family, and we who were once not His people were made His people through the blood of Jesus. ***You see, the blessing distinguishes you.*** Psalm 68:19 says, His blessings daily loads us up with benefits. What God blesses is blessed forever. When God confers a blessing, it is permanent. The word "confer" means to grant a title, degree, benefit, right or privilege. So God has given us the right to prosper, the benefit of His power and the privilege of living above and being the top. Privilege means an advantage, immunity or access that is available to a certain person or group based on a common factor such as heritage or resource. So we are blessed by God because the Word says that He blesses His people and who He blesses is blessed forever.

We now know that the word "forever" means forever. We now walk with an advantage and benefit from the blessing daily. It is available to us. We have to become aware of it and expect it to operate in our lives daily. If we believe and speak it, the blessing will be activated and God will perform miracles. The blessing will replenish, restore, and recover everything in our lives. It may not look like a garden, but you can make it a garden. You can create it wherever you go, designed to live from the inside out. You are designed to be **Powerful, Prominent, Preserved, Prosperous, Perceptive, and Proficient.** When the blessing is at work, the curse is reversed and the blessing cannot be revoked. The Bible says what God has blessed, no man can curse. It also says, the blessing produces rain in its season along with provision, safety, and grace. The blessing produces the supernatural enabling to get wealth and makes one rich without pain or toil.

When the blessing is at work, all your enemies are destroyed. Utterly, they will be destroyed because God has blessed us and no one can curse us. Even our offspring, our children are blessed because of the blessing at work.

YOU WERE MADE FOR MORE

There was a woman in the Bible named Naomi, who lost her husband and sons. Because of these loses, she felt compelled to send her daughter-in-laws away out of a desire for them to find happiness. She judged herself and her situation as dead because of the deaths that have occurred in her life. However, one of the in-laws, Ruth, refused to go because she knew the source of her blessing. Ruth knew that one of the fruits of Naomi's womb was once her blessing. This fruit became her husband and provided her with protection, provision, shelter and satisfaction. Ruth understood that going back where she was before had little or no chance of success. In fact, this is why she left in the first place. That is why she was there. It is the same within our lives. When we have failures in our lives often we are challenged to go back to the old, what used to be, but the voice telling you to go back is not "protective." It might sound legit. It may just truly be trying to be protective, but it is about to cut you off from the blessing. It may be the voice in your head. It may be your "mamma and them." Whoever it is, it's not of God. God says keep on going. You started towards me, keep on going. Oprah, the other daughter-in-law turned back, but Ruth did not.

Ruth knew she was made for more - more than loss, more than bitterness, more than nothingness, more than lack, more than not enough, and more than unrealized dreams. And you are made for more.

When Naomi gave her daughter-in-laws her ultimatum, Ruth replied, *"Where you go, I will go, and where you stay, I will stay. Your people will be my people and your God my God. Where you die I will die, and there I will be buried. May the LORD deal with me, be it ever so severely, if even death separates you and me. When Naomi realized that Ruth was determined to go with her, she stopped urging her. So the two women went on until they came to Bethlehem. When they arrived in Bethlehem, the whole town was stirred because of them, and the women exclaimed, "Can this be Naomi?"'*

They may talk about you when you change your mind, change your course, change your friends, or let things go. You may even at times look defeated, like you lost, but stay the course; it is almost harvest time for you.

5 THINGS THAT WILL ACTIVATE THE BLESSING

1) **Know** the source of your blessing. Ruth was married and lived with her husband's family. All died except the mother-in-law. Ruth knew who the producer was. Her mother–in-law had been successful in the past.

2) **Partner** with someone you can learn from and give strength to. Partnership gives and takes.

3) **Submit** to the redeemer. Boaz was her husband's kin and by custom the one who could buy Ruth back. Jesus is our Redeemer.

4) **Follow** a producer. Her mother-in-law had produced three sons and was the producer of her husband's first success. She followed her.

5) **Gather** the leftovers. In any field there is more thrown away, unused, or left behind. You don't have to fight for what others have, just find and gather the leftovers.

The blessing was spoken by God toward us in Genesis 1:28. We connect with the blessing by acknowledging God as the Creator and source of the blessing, which releases the blessing into our lives and the abundance God originally intended for man. The blessing is the promise to prosper. You've heard a man going to the father of the bride and asking for his blessing to marry his daughter. It's the same deal. The blessing is an allowance to produce the desired intent. In our culture while it is used loosely, the blessing is the bestowing of favor on another to increase, be fruitful, abound, and be well.

"Bless you" is said automatically when someone sneezes or when the candidate makes speeches, they confer a blessing on the United States of America. So the blessing is the permission to increase, prosper, multiply, replenish, control, subdue, and always be on top. In Genesis 2, the scriptures record how God made the earth and the Garden of Eden (with all its provisions), and then placed man in the center of it.

God gave man the assignment of tending and caring for the garden. Why? I believe that each of us needs work assignments, a way of creating as we are in the image and likeness of God. When Adam was made, the earth had everything he needed. That's the blessing at work. When Adam needed a companion without him asking, God knew what he had need of and made him a wife or help meet. That's the blessing at work.

In Matthew 6:33, when Jesus says, *"Seek ye first the kingdom of God and its righteousness and all these things will be added to you,"* that's the blessing at work. When the Bible says in Proverbs, *"The blessing of the Lord makes rich and adds no sorrow"* that's the blessing at work. When Ephesians says, *"We are his workmanship created in his image unto good works,"* that's the blessing at work. When God made a covenant with Abraham and said I will bless you and your posterity, the blessing caused him to be so great that he had 318 servants that were born into his household. That doesn't count the parents or children of those servants or the other servants not born in that household. That's the blessing at work. When the Bible describes Abraham's son, Jacob, it says he was **very** great. He had **great** riches. That's the blessing at work. But the blessings wouldn't stop.

When Abraham's descendants would have died in a famine, He allowed Joseph to be delivered into the hands of Egyptians, then He promoted him from the pit to the palace -- up to the highest level of Egyptian rule, second only to Pharaoh. In so doing, God ensured the survival of Abraham's descendants and gave them the resources that they would live. That's like your enemy putting you in a place of honor. That's the blessing at work.

When the children of a Jewish descendant would have perished due to their enemies plot against them, God raised up Esther and placed her in a position of honor and favor to deliver them and give them protection. Listen, God will do the same for His children. You are in a position of favor with the King. That's the blessing at work.

The deliverance from Babylonian captivity, that's the blessing at work. When the fullness of time had come and God sent His Son, born of a woman, that's the blessing at work. When you received Jesus as Lord of your life, that's the blessing at work. When you picked up this book, that's the blessing at work.

God is calling you. The blessing is at work right now. It is shifting your thoughts, expectations, and beliefs. In Him we have obtained an inheritance. That's the blessing at work. When I came again to the Lord, I began to see what the truth of God's revealed Word said about me.

The blessing is the enabling power of God to excel and to rise above every circumstance and every situation that Satan has tried to use to hold us back or to keep us down.

The first thing I understood was that the Word said I was righteous in Christ Jesus, and by faith I received the Word, so I renewed my mind. It is extremely difficult to believe that you are made right when all of our lives we are told we are wrong. In a world where every mistake is counted against you, it's difficult to believe that all our sins, God remembers no more and our faults are not counted against us. But I labored to rest in His word. I read it, confessed it, meditated on it and received it. Then the blessing started to work.

What is the blessing? The blessing is the power of God to produce, increase, reproduce and multiply. The blessing is the enabling power of God to excel and to rise above every circumstance and every situation that Satan has tried to use to hold us back or to keep us down. It makes every situation end in our favor. The blessing makes everything work together for our good. The blessing allows us to be on top when the "smoke clears." It makes us a conqueror. It takes us into situation and brings us out with the spoils of the enemy.

The blessing (as it is given to Abraham and his seed) is a legal binding contract that is unchanging and final. Everyone who is Abraham's seed is in this contract. This blessing has caused me to triumph in every situation, every attack, and every attempt to destroy me have been foiled or worked in my favor because the blessing is at work. Look, every situation is different and the same need may call for a different result, but God does not fail. The blessing doesn't fail. Religion fails, our limited thinking fails, our carnal mind fails, but God never, ever ever fails!

Since I believe in and received by faith from the Word of God about how God sees me, then I was able to believe and receive what the Word said about what He has done for me. You see, it is easy for us to believe that God is righteous, good, and just, and we can even easily believe God is merciful and loving. However, to believe that God will bless us or that we deserve the blessing because we are in Christ, and that we will be blessed in every situation goes against everything that we were taught (especially those) that are taught by the church, but the Word says that we are joint-heirs with Christ.

In Revelation 1, it tells us what Jesus is entitled to, what His inheritance is and as joint-heirs it means we also are possessors of this wealth. Oftentimes people talk themselves out of or walk away from their blessing because they seek to understand it in the natural or predict with their limited minds what the outcome might be. If they feel bad, they claim sickness. If the doctor agrees with a diagnosis, there is confirmation. If they have financial lack or job loss, they begin to agree with the economist and others that there is a global economic depression or recession. Those of us who have revelation of the Word know there is no loss in Christ, no lack, just gain and increase. What looked like loss is a set up. What looks like a lack is the glory of God. Whatever is going on is to reveal God by taking away all other power, so that no man may glory.

I waited and believed from 1999 through 2006 to see the overflow financial downfall of God in my life. I was waiting for the tsunami blessing to overtake me and cause the glory of God to be revealed again and the more. The blessing is like water; it will go everywhere, seep through every crack and crevice and wet or overtake everything. If you believe God and expect the goodness of God to show up in your life, it will. If you don't get weary of believing and if you don't give up on God's goodness, you will see it. Here's the crux of the matter; I know you believe God is good, but you must also believe that He is a rewarder and that you deserve the reward.

Grace is the unmerited, undeserved favor of God. Of course it is. But because of what Jesus did, God's grace has made you righteous through faith. Now you stand in right relationship with God. You are right before God and therefore entitled to be rewarded. God is a good master. He is full of compassion. Jesus because of His obedience has caused the blessing to come on you. He has caused you (in Him) to deserve the blessing. If you see yourself as not deserving the blessing, then you will interpret your situation as a loss, as failure. If you see yourself as God's righteousness, God's child, an heir of God the Father, joint-heirs with Christ, then you can expect, predict, and declare the blessing in every situation. The blessing is at work in every situation.

Psalm 105 recalls the history of God's favor and God's faithfulness. It ends with the explanation of why God did those mighty acts for the Hebrews. It was because of His covenant promise to Abraham. It tells that God brought out Abraham's people with rejoicing and shouts of joy, and that they inherited what others have toiled to attain. The result of this will be to the praise and glory of God. Psalm 107 says that the redeemed, the saved, the delivered, the exalted ones tell this story of the Lord's mighty acts and it ends with this advice: let those that are wise listen and consider the living ways of the Lord. It is my desire that the redeemed will tell the story about how the blessing is at work in their lives and how it works every time.

The Blessing Connector

Now, the ability to understand, accept and apply this next principle is essential to the blessing God gave us through Jesus Christ. God made us and consequently understands our working. He who made us and works through us also created a system for us that will cause us to have control and power to have a God life. In Genesis 2:17, God said to the man, do not eat from the tree of the knowledge of good and evil for if you do, you will certainly die. God gave man the fruit of every tree in the garden except one. Just like our income, God gave us the free use of all of it except the tithe (10% of our income). Adam and Eve ate of the fruit and God stated His promise to them after they disobeyed saying, from dust you came to dust you shall return. The blessing that was spoken over man by God in Genesis 1:20 was the blessing of increase, multiplication, fruitfulness, and rule. There was only one instruction that God gave that would cancel the blessing. If you eat from this tree, you will die.

Now, my revelation on the tithe is this, when you understand that you are in relationship with the Almighty God who created heaven and earth, and that He owns all the silver and gold, and He has control of all the resources of the earth, and He will not withhold any good thing from you, then this knowledge will allow the abundance to be seen and there will be no lack.

Lack is a condition that is only real when seen, acknowledged or acted upon. When God made the earth, He made it with enough resources to feed all mankind. That's why He put the fishes in the sea, birds in the air, livestock and animals on the land, and seed bearing plants and trees to have fruit with seed in it. Lack was introduced by the serpent when he said to the woman, if you eat the fruit you will have something you are currently without. Here is how it is recorded in Genesis 3:5, *"For God knows that when you eat from it your eyes will be opened and you will be like God knowing good and evil."*

The evil one, like he did in the garden, identified lack to us by saying we don't have enough to honor God with our tithe, but when we agree, we begin to live that reality *"of not enough,"* always eating the fruit of our labor with the seed in it until it leads to death.

The Bible says that God gives seed to the sower. When we sow, God will supply and multiply our seeds for sowing. If your seed for sowing is multiplied, your fruit from an abundant harvest is multiplied. The seed is a small part of the larger fruit, which is for eating. This scriptural reference found in 2 Corinthians 9 begins with the writer of Corinthians,

Apostle Paul, encouraging us to sow generously that we might reap generously.

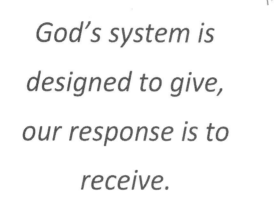

God's system is designed to give, our response is to receive.

In verse 11, Paul says the sower will be enriched in every way so that he can be generous on every occasion and his generosity will result in thanksgiving to God. As much as we have (like in the Garden of Eden), we are real experts on locating what is missing and cursing what we have as not enough. As much as we have, we are willing to eat the one thing that will not feed us or make a difference in our financial situation. It's amazing how we are willing to exchange our money for shoes, cars, or whatever, but we are not willing to exchange a tithe for more money.

Now, I know that this is difficult for many people because too many people have used the truth of God's Word to take from others. Tithing is an act where the tither gets more not taken advantage of. Too many people have been taught that the earth has limited resources. Too many have been taught a system founded on greed. You know the take all you can system, hold all you have system or to steal what you need system.

People are no longer looking for assignments. They are only going after money/provision rather than purpose. Translation: Going after the most lucrative jobs/opportunities, keeping it all for yourself, lying on your taxes, and not doing what your employer is paying you to do. But the Bible says in Matthew, Chapter 6:33, seek first the kingdom of God and His system and all the things you seek after will be added to you.

God's system is designed to give, our response is to receive. His system gives us ways to receive and increase. I believe it is such an important principle and this is why the enemy has really done all he could to deceive, destroy, and devastate this truth. He tricked Eve into giving up the blessing, and continues to do it to some, even to this day. You "gotta" ask yourself, if I keep the tithe will I become rich? If I become rich what does it profit me if I'm not found in faith in God?

In 1999, when Pastor Holice Robertson first introduced me to the study of God's Word, I fell hard, fast, and completely in love with Jesus. The revelation of His immeasurable love for me and His insatiable desire towards my good was mind shifting. I became sold out to the service of the Lord. Later through my own study, I found scriptures on tithing and giving to God, and just like every other principle in the Word, I operated in it.

The first eye opener God gave me on tithing was the scripture found in Genesis of Abraham giving to Melchizedek after a battle. You see, Abraham fought five kings and won. He took their goods, people, and wealth. Then he met a priest named Melchizedek and without commandment or law, Abraham gave a tithe to this priest. Abraham understood that God was his only source and that God had given him the victory in battle. Deeper still, Abraham somehow knew that he had a never ending, limitless source and that giving would not take away, it would only speak of his reliance on the one true God. God said to Abraham, "I am your shield and exceeding great reward." Abraham wanted God more than he wanted stuff. With my faith built on the Word that God was my more than a great reward, I walked in the desire to only please Him. Now, I have to confess in these early days, I did not know about the promises associated with giving. I just loved God and wanted to do whatever God said.

Since Abraham was called the father of our faith and since the Bible says faith pleases God (without faith it is impossible to please God), I studied Abraham's actions. After a while of studying, God revealed to me the promises associated with tithing. Recorded in Malachi 3, God said, He would open the windows of heaven and pour us out a blessing we won't have room enough to receive. God told me that to prove something is to test the statement or its truth. Proving is the evidence of it. God said to me by this you can prove I am real and my Word is the truth. He said I am active, and I am a good God, not only to you, but also to unbelievers.

I know God existed, that he loved me, and that he was good. I told God I didn't need any further proof, my spirit was regenerated. I knew Him in my Spirit. I believed on the One He sent. Then God said I want others to know what you know. I want to demonstrate my faithfulness through you. I want it not for you, but for those who haven't believed. Now, that's the same thing I wanted, for God's love to become known.

So I began to tithe with the expectation that I would receive a blessing that I wouldn't have room enough to receive. I gave to speak of my allegiance to God. I gave to honor God. I gave in recognition of God having given it to me. I gave to present my body (the time and energy I exchange for money) as a living sacrifice. But as I gave, my finances began to diminish. It just seemed like there came more need than ever before and less money than ever before. The more I gave, the less I had. The enemy came after me with fierceness. You see the more I spoke of God's ability, the more the devil assigned demons to attack my finances. It became so disheartening that while I continued to tithe, it became difficult for me to say what God said will happen if you give.

For a while the devil tried to dry up my expectation, shame me, and shut my mouth. He knew that the only way to disconnect me was to show me what was not available. He tried to shut my giving down. Regardless, I held fast to tithing. I didn't quit. I would've give in even though it seemed like I was not going to see God move in my finances. But because I read the Word, I held fast to the Word. I filled myself with the Word concerning finances: Give and it shall be given to you, and that it was more blessed to give than to receive.

I believed God, and against all hope, I hoped in God. I declared that God was true, that His Words have power and will perform. I held on and was determined. When the truth was fully formed in me, the lie of lack could not stand. When the lie called lack could not stop me from tithing or shut my mouth that God through Jesus had provided for all liberally, lack shriveled up and ran away. Then the

The blessing is a supernatural empowerment to produce without stress. It is the ability to multiply and increase in resources, and to replenish the earth.

proof of God's great provision that was in me overflowed out of me and into every area of my life to an exceeding abundance. I can't convince you of this truth, I can only challenge you to prove Him yourself. Lots of people give what they have. That's not a tithe. Lots of others give an offering. That's not a tithe. The word tithe means 10%.

Then some people who give a tithe are giving without an expectation. Others are hoping for financial increase, but speaking negative words over their seed and condition, or a wealthy person's condition. Sow with expectation, with a good word, and don't ever stop.

The blessing of the Lord makes us rich and it adds no toil, labor or grief to it. The blessing is a supernatural empowerment to produce without stress. It is the ability to multiply and increase in resources, and to replenish the earth. It is a power to subdue and control things and rule over the earth. It is a supernatural ability to always win and be on top.

God gave us the power to get wealth so that He can establish His covenant that He swore to Abraham. Expect the blessing of financial increase. Give to the local church 10% of your income (if you have to ask gross or net, you are not ready to believe God). Speak the Word of God concerning your giving. Expect God to be faithful to His word and receive the blessings and increase that comes from the Lord. Without tithing and offering, there's no way (that I know) to connect you to the blessing of financial increase.

I have heard people say I have given a lot of tithe and nothing happened. If you believe that then nothing will happen. Also, saying that the preacher is taking your seed or judging whether or not it's good ground is like a farmer pulling his seed up after sowing it and burning it, but still believing it will bring forth a harvest.

Speaking against your seed in your life saying that you are broke or busted will cause it to be. Give and receive, God has a bountiful supply as you give. Receive it in your spirit. The Word of God declares give and it shall be given. Not might, but shall. As you give believe the Word and receive a good measure, shaken together and running over into your life blessing (Luke 6:38).

4 Types of Giving

Tithe: Giving for God's purpose. Malachi 3 says bring the tithes and offering into the storehouse so that there will be meat in my house and prove me now.

First Fruit: First Fruit is giving for your purpose which is to honor God for His blessing in you. There are 31 references throughout the Bible about the first fruits. If the first fruits be holy then the rest is holy. Roman 11:16 says first fruits are an acknowledgement of what God has done. It's traditionally given after the harvest to honor God as the source.

Alms: Giving is for the purpose of helping mankind. Alms are for helping others. In Proverbs 19:17 it says, he who gives to the poor lends to the Lord and God will pay back what is given. There is no promise at rebuking the devourer for our sake in alms giving. You can't take first fruits or alms and think of it as tithing. It is not a substitute for tithing. It is a different thing.

Seed – Matthew 4:8 says seed giving and offering is the way the 30, 60, or 100 fold is received. Seed stops poverty and brings harvest. The seed accomplishes the impossible.

Prosperity is the growth or advancement towards the desired end. The advancement of the Kingdom of God is done through believers. Prosperity can happen in any season, any place, any territory, and any geographic location. The greatest command for any believer is to go into the world and preach the gospel. I like what St. Francis of Assisi said, "Preach the gospel at all time, use words if necessary." It is in moments of crisis and unbelievable conditions that we can get people's attention and then show them Christ in the crisis. I'm not discounting the fact that people walk through different seasons, but what I am saying is that whatever you are in, can get better. The kingdom of God can prosper and advance in any location. You can grow and advance to your desired end no matter what you face.

Wealth Transfer

Ok, I know you've seen moguls working extreme hours. Unjust men just attracted to working for money. They work to exhaustion just to make more money than others. I know what this is. They are preparing for the wealth transfer.

In Ecclesiastes 2:26, the word says, *"To the person who pleases him, God gives wisdom, knowledge and happiness, but to the sinner he gives the task of gathering and storing up wealth to hand it over to the one who pleases God."* Did you see that? The sinners' job is to work hard collecting and storing wealth to be handed over to the righteous. That's wealth transfer.

Wealth transfer is not only from sinner to righteous. In Proverbs 13:22, it says, a good man leaves an inheritance for his children's children; and the wealth of the sinner is laid up for the just. So a good man transfers wealth to his children and grandchildren. They have to acquire the money to be transferred to the righteous.

In Deuteronomy 28:12 and 13, we are supposed to lend to many nations and not borrow; we are to be the head and not the tail. Does this sound like you currently? The only way to achieve it is by earning, laboring, or grace. Grace is the supernatural enablement to produce beyond your ability. That is the wealth transfer. We don't work for increase. We work for fulfillment of divine purpose. When we work according to His purpose, we are valuable; we enrich the earth and the inhabitants of the earth responds by giving us the resources necessary or equal to fulfilling our purpose as received by us in our spirit.

Our purpose is inside of us and as we produce our purpose, it will propel us to the wealthy place where the transfer of wealth will happen. The Bible says in Proverbs 10, that the blessings of the Lord produce wealth without toil. The Bible says do not work for increase. It's not that you shouldn't work to eat, but don't work without the divine purpose of God in mind.

No matter what work I did, I was conscious that God had me there for a reason and a season and that my work wasn't for increase, but to advance the kingdom of God as well as be a good manager of what He sent into my life.

Every problem, I saw as an opportunity. Every disaster, I looked at it the same way. It was a small thing to God. You see, even if we were to gain wealth through hard work, it would be temporal. After we die, it would not matter. It would not be eternal. It will rust; it is subject to thieves. But when we get wealth through God's power and for God's purpose, we do more than receive financial wealth;

Our purpose is inside of us and as we produce our purpose, it will propel us to the wealthy place where the transfer of wealth will happen.

we will also affect others and accomplish an eternal purpose. The Bible depicts a number of wealth transfers. Notable amongst them are the children of Israel taking the Egyptians' wealth when they left Egypt led by Moses. Another one was when Abram fought five kings that banded together against him, but with the help of God, he prevailed and took all their stuff with him. Also, Jacob took Laban's wealth when it was time for him to leave Laban's house. And lastly, Joseph was given charge of everything in Egypt along with being chosen to be second in command to Pharaoh.

Isaiah 46:9, talks about how God's works are traceable in the spirit, but not in the natural. It says the natural mind cannot perceive God. The man whose eyes are fixed on God, is the only one the works of God will be revealed to. Accessing the wealth transfer will have to start with the spirit first. We must first believe what God says: We must leave an inheritance; we will be the head and not the tail; and we will be the lender and not the borrower.

LIES AND TRUTHS

Now that your thoughts are on God's promises rather than on your circumstances, on the harvest rather than the seed, it is time for you to look at the promises, principles and precepts of wealth transfer. Remember, stay in the promise and not in the result as we progress through this segment, and know that God has not given us the spirit of Fear.

Fear is the spirit intended to create a boundary and rob you from the possibility of expanding your borders. But you don't have to do anything, but believe that God is able to make every grace, every favor and every earthly blessings come to you.

God made man with three parts: spirit, soul and body. It is with the spirit that everything will operate from. The soul will be used to retrieve, process and interpret information. Lastly, the body will be the place where everything resides and be acted out. Like a physical location where those who live in it are housed, so your spirit and your purpose are in you waiting you to act it out in your body. The eternal, unconquerable, unimaginable, incomprehensible genius of God is in us. It's who we are, three in one to be an ultimate creative force on earth. We are made for greatness. Hardwired to produce outcomes, programmed to win, called to dominate, conquer, multiply and increase.

II Corinthians tells us that we do not look at temporary things, but the things that are eternal. In order to create the kind of faith that moves mountains, you have to start seeing and visualizing the invisible promises of God being your birthright. Put your eyes on the harvest. Abram had to use the stars to see the promise that his descendants will be many and that he would be the father of many nations. Joshua had to see himself winning the battle as a mighty warrior before he won it (Joshua 1:8).

Joseph saw himself being powerful and the head before it happened. He didn't know how it was going to happen, but the Bible says man plans his way, but God directs his steps. While you are working and creating the picture in your mind based on God's Word, Satan is working on an alternative picture in your mind. He can only work by challenging the promise of God from coming true in your life by causing you to focus on your past or present. Proverbs 4:23 says, out of <u>the issue of</u> your heart flows the issue of life. It's time to refresh the image.

Your "IP address" has to change. The image of God must constantly be in your heart. The image of the all-knowing, all-powerful, all mighty, all in control, all in all God should be in your heart; it will produce.

The Bible says out of the abundance of the heart, the mouth speaks. Psalm 39:1, reminds us to bridle our tongue. When we look at the promise and then look at/consider where we are, sometimes we get faithless. Remember, as a man thinks in his heart, so is he. We can't see how we can get there, but the promise is only to be believed. Therefore, we must meditate on the Word of God both day and night (Psalm 1), then eventually, if you believe (really believe), you will begin to act on it and speak it.

Usually we are speaking and acting out our daily needs and not our belief in God for the covenant promise to come to pass. In Matthew 26:9, the disciples said about the woman putting the ointment on Jesus, you should sell that and give it to the poor. There is going to be people along the way (border bullies) that will speak against you. People (even Christians) whose minds are un-renewed and who are deceived, who believe that there is a limited amount of resources on the planet. These bullies will attempt to railroad you, stockpile you, and shame you through accusations, innuendos, and attacks. This is especially hurtful for those of us who desire to be helpful, meaningful, and above reproach. But I tell you the truth, they did it to Jesus.

Even the most brilliant economist will tell you that there's a limited supply because they are looking at the world's system and the things that already created and how it has already produced. They see a limited supply; a limited supply of the world's resources, so they assume that if we get more, we will be taking it from someone else rather than increase through an exchange. This system is dependent on increase through taking away. However, we are in Christ as new creatures washed in the blood created under God for good works.

The disciples thought that the anointing oil used for God's purpose would be better spent on the poor rather than understanding everything is made for God's purpose. You see, we receive the wealth transfer for God's purpose: to win souls, to preach the Gospel, to be fishers of men, and to allow God to establish His covenant with us that he may be proven true and faithful to His word He swore to Abraham, Isaac and Jacob. The enemy wants you to keep focusing on your past or present. He tries to keep you out of the wealthy place by causing you to think, who am I to have this wealth and to live this well. I am doing something wrong or dirty to be living this rich and in the flow of God's best. But in Jesus' name, we come against every thought, imagination or feeling that exalts itself against the knowledge of Jesus Christ. The blessing of the Lord is on you, for you, and with you. Be fruitful; be glad for the abundance of all things (Deuteronomy 28).

WHILE YOU WAIT

1) **Meditate** on the word of God both day and night. By doing this, it will get down into your heart because when you believe it; you will say as David said in the Bible, "I believe it so."

2) **Declare** the Word of God at all times. Whatever you say, you will have what you want, so say the will of God, say what God says. When believing and speaking is in operation at once, that's a partnership.

3) **Partnership** is the working together of two or more. Learn how it feels to serve another person's vision. For more than 11 years, I faithfully served the vision of my Pastor, Holice Robertson. His vision to create a place where the love of God is evident, the Word of God is being taught and the Spirit of God is directing. You can find this principle in many places in the Bible. David and Saul, Naomi and Ruth, Moses and Joshua are just a few of the Bile characters that demonstrate partnership and service of another's vision that led to the servant's promotion. Until you've served another's vision, you will not be ready to serve your own vision and you will not be able to draw others to serve your vison. Seek to partner with other believers, other visionaries; others who celebrate you not tolerate you. Partner with those who are hungry

for what you are hungry for and confident in their success. Someone said show me your friends and I will show you your future.

God blessed me with a twin sister that not only celebrates me, but, gets me. To me, we are different, yet, we get each other. I wouldn't do what she does. She wouldn't do what I do, but we get how and why each other does the things we do. We are hungry for God's righteousness to be revealed and be found in us. We hunger for the Word and for the ways of God. We hunger for great success that the will of God and the glory of God can be manifested. We empathize and hope for the best for each other. We support and are loyal to each other and through her eyes, I see she loves me and believes in me. I can accomplish the task and win the race. I run with her because she is running, too.

Another partner that has been instrumental in my development is my husband, Courtney Munroe. I see the love my husband has for me reflected in the environment we have in our home. I was fortunate to marry the most ethical, moral, and giving man. He is my best friend and over 20 years I've hung out with him more than with anyone else, and although I was a good citizen person, his standard of morality has increased my moral standards considerably. From the minor things like show up without excuse. If you made a plan to be there, show up on time every time. He is bound by his word and seeks to act in ways that are of the highest caliber. He is respectful and loving, and has high expectations of others. While I believed in social justice, equality and fairness; and I championed the cause of the underdog, he through his daily commitments have showed me that keeping my word, being on time, living in excellence and putting my household first is important, too. He also taught me that doing the little things right mattered as much as doing the big things. He taught me to care about the day to day stuff and to be careful over the little.

4) **Be a good steward** or building up to a breakthrough. Doing the right thing consistently in everything is what we must strive to do such as going to work every day on time; working as unto the Lord. When it's easy and when it's not. No matter how it looks or how it feels; no matter who can see you or what they think. Years ago, I was in a little green house on an obscure road in a little town (there is a lesson and a preparation that can only happen in obscurity). Unknown, uncelebrated, un-thanked, but I worked with the 12 children God entrusted to me. I worked diligently and consistently as if I was on America's best and was responsible for teaching the world how to be the best child care provider. I worked as unto God. I worked with the constant realization that God had given me every thing, every child, every minute as an opportunity not for me, but caring for His property.

I loved and cared for "God's little ones" like they were the president's children. In fact, in my heart, I saw them as the kids of the King of kings and that God had sent them to me to develop on the backside in the hidden valley to strengthen them for their special life assignment. I felt extremely blessed by them. I also took care of the dingy, little, run down property. I constantly picked up, straightened up and tidied up. Looking in on, it might have looked comical or very sad to the naked eye. A seemingly capable over qualified, well spoken, well-read individual caring for 12 children below market cost. In a small, dilapidated, DIY renovated, previously bank foreclosed house…but God!

Some of the children had high needs. Some of the parents couldn't pay. Some wouldn't come on time. Some children spent some nights at the center. Some parents came troubled and without much hope. Sometimes we had to counsel them and be their friend, but no matter what was required, every service was done in love and with excellence. I understand now that while the work was physically exhausting, I was not tired at all because of the way I thought about that work. I thought that God had assigned me to that work, so I was inspired and motivated to do the work for God. You see, your thinking can cause you to operate in a freedom which would allow you to surpass limitations and boundaries.

Look at your little situation as God's opportunity.

> *Look at your little situation as God's opportunity. A miracle can only happen if there is a need. If it is not enough, it is ripe for a miracle.*

A miracle can only happen if there is a need. If it is not enough, it is ripe for a miracle. Trust God and while you are there, take care of what God has given you. Show love, act excellently with what you have. You have to act at all times as if someone is watching. Truth: He is.

Do you have a little more? Manage it well. Don't use it outside of what you absolutely need it for. Do you have a little faith, use it to pray and read the Bible. Do you have a little house, take care of it and treat it like the big house you are hoping for. I'm not asking you to do anything. I'm asking you to see yourself on a journey with God and that the reason you are in that situation is that God has called you to it to take care of it for Him. It is not yours, it is God's. I worked 12 hour days, then I went home with my husband, my two year old son and six year old daughter and took care of them. I did this for five years faithfully.

5) **STEP OUT IN FAITH-** Faith is the foundation from which all these ingredients flow out of. Without faith it is impossible to please God. We must

believe not only that God exists, but also that He is a rewarder of them that diligently seek Him.

Be found in faith -- doing business until He comes. Recognition is the key. You must recognize what is in your life. Recognize everything that's happening at this moment that God is setting you up. Many times people recognize the burden and lack rather than recognizing that in the same situation there is actual gain and victory. If it didn't work the way you expected, you gained information. If someone rejects you that is gain for you to know, that door wasn't for you, that relationship wasn't meant to be. If someone betrays you that's gain for you. You have a better understanding about how to treat people and what people expect from you. If you lose the job that is gain for you. You know that job was not for you. Whatever happened, it means that those people who have mistreated you has propelled you forward if you would receive the wisdom in the failure. So it would not be a failure, but a gain. I'm telling you, you are gaining. You cannot fail. Your haters are indeed the cheerleaders; the secret agents come to promote you to end a season and to provide you with direction and elevation.

Haters truly are the best evidence that you are succeeding. No hater has much to do with hindering people who are not threatening to break out and live well. If there are people who without cause is troubling or hindering you; it is your witness that you are coming out. Faith allows you to see yourself and your situation as good and purposed by God. It allows you to act well and hopeful at all times. Faith causes you to believe the best at all times. Faith is what one sows when there is nothing but hope.

6) **Sow**: Sowing is an essential agreement to the recipe. It's like the baking powder in the cake – the ingredient that you are not able to eat alone. It may not taste as good as the sugar, frosting, butter or milk, but it is very necessary to the expected result. How do I know, because I have proven God's faithfulness in this? I remember

when I started to tithe; I gave twenty eight dollars a week.

One day, after several months of tithing my husband asked me if I knew what tithe meant. When I responded that it was 10 percent, he then said well twenty eight dollars is more than 10 percent. I knew that, but I didn't want to just give exactly a tithe. I wanted to give an offering, too. I was so grateful for what I had been given on the cross, and for the opportunity to give to further the gospel. I was excited to prove God and to obey His Word. I added about ten dollars every week as offering.

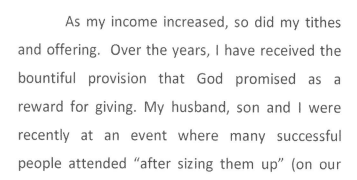

Sowing positions you for promotion. The Bible says your gift will bring you before great men.

As my income increased, so did my tithes and offering. Over the years, I have received the bountiful provision that God promised as a reward for giving. My husband, son and I were recently at an event where many successful people attended "after sizing them up" (on our way home), my son remarked that he was unimpressed with the professional achievements of the other attendees. He noted that I was more successful financially although I did not have their superior education and connections. He then concluded that my success must be from God because they went to better schools had more opportunity, but none of them were as successful.

You see, sowing positions you for promotion. The Bible says your gift will bring you before great men. Sometimes when it feels like you don't have enough, fear can overwhelm you and cause you to not do what you want to. When this happens to me, I not only pray, and say God's Word, but I stay focus, by developing a plan that I could follow. I always fight fear with a plan.

I told you earlier that I am believing God to be debt free so that can sometimes present fear of the expectation being unfulfilled, so I follow this plan.

1)   I get a vision and a goal and write it down. I make a vision board. I want to be debt free, so I've written it down. I've

also created a vision board full of pictures of what my life would look like when I'm debt free. There are women celebrating, jumping for joy, writing books and holding conferences on debt freedom. There is a pile of cash and a car. These images represent how I see me in my debt free future. Use this example, if you want to be debt free, write the vision. How would it look in your life, if it would be fulfilled? What would change? Maybe your mailbox wouldn't run over with bills or maybe you would be able to give to that charity or provide for your family better. If so, write down how you want it to be.

2)   Next, I calculate all of my debts and make that the sum of money that I am believing for.

3)   Add it up. Find out what you make, what your debt is, and where the rest is going. Take stock of it. There are extras that you

currently have that are being wasted and begin to use that to affect debt.

4) Have a plan and everyday for 20 minutes work the plan. It can take many routes. You can call creditors and design a custom payment plan, which includes elimination or reduction of the total debt or interest rate. It may be praying over the bills or declaring the Word over it. It may be studying the Word concerning debt and freedom. It could be engaging in enterprise that would increase your income. Yearn to be debt free.

5) Work to increase your passion and revelation of the vision for your finances. Save three to six months' worth of paychecks. It can happen by first agreeing this is a desire in your life. Don't reject it by saying, I can't even pay my bills, how can I save. Just receive it as a *desire.* Then study and pray the Word over saving and financial increase.

6) Educate yourself in the area of finances. Read additional material, take online courses, find information as well as study the US economic system. Increase or grow your understanding.

7) Always sow seed for the goal. Your offering should have direction. Sow your offering with your goal for your finances in mind and speak over it when you are sowing it. Tell it what it will return as.

From the time I decided to be rich, it was "I need to get money to help others." I saw addressing the needs of children or vulnerable people as a real passion. I had a serious penchant for the underdog. It was not so much that I identified with the underdog so much as I identified with the hero. Don't get me wrong, I know my compassion senses are overdeveloped. I even cry when another hurts. I can hardly watch certain shows even movies without crying. My empathetic nerve is very sensitized. But I just don't feel sad for pain, I also feel called to action. That feeling can cause me to want to build houses even though that is outside of my skill-set. This happened often when I owned the daycare.

At some point the business took so much time and mental effort that I became single minded about its prosperity and success. There were many threats to the success of the organization both external and internal that I became caught up in; sacrifice after sacrifice of my time and energy, and as a result, relationships suffered. However, I was fortunate to have a very supportive and stable primary family. My husband and children adored me almost as much as I adored them. My life with them had always been whole, happy, one of full acceptance, mutual respect, and admiration. I loved them and I loved people. My husband and children knew this and honored this passion, so there was no disconnect or confusion with them. When a project took most of my time, they made the adjustment and encouraged me. They knew I was driven and I loved that about me.

However I did feel a sense of guilt as I put the needs of the business ahead of them. As the business prospered and was doing well and I could afford much, it became about me and my family getting opportunities and investing in our growth and stability. Other times, it was about making up for what they lost to the business.

Then the self-actualization happened and a sense of being lost imposed itself in my spirit -- a ship with no direction, no purpose. How many restaurants could I eat out at? How many indulgences? Another moment of transition was taking place. And ironically, it was painful and confusing. All of a sudden, what seemed to be what I was after, what I should be enjoying became a valley place.

Mountain top experiences have to start there. I was hurting for what I was made for. I had no one that had achieved my level of success; no one to turn to. I couldn't understand the deep pain and longing I felt.

Through prayer, God would lead me to different pieces of understanding, prisms of light until He showed me that I had lost the reason I went after the prosperity. Prosperity, He reminded me was the means; the end was to help others, contributing to their needs. Oh, sure, throughout the years, I would give generously to charitable organizations, including the local homeless shelter (The Durham Rescue Mission), Goodwill Industries, and my church, but the pain was still there. I also was giving to national and international Christian ministries. I gave to friends and family in need or in trouble. I created jobs for friends and family and for community members who had no job, sometimes no experience and no opportunity. However, the specific reason for the wealth acquisition was to use the resources to address needs of the most vulnerable citizens in my community and around the world. I had engaged in such a battle for the business that at some point that struggle became the focus and the prosperity became my reward to soothe the guilt and isolation I felt.

When God answered my cry and reminded me about my original intent, I realized the reason for the pain was the purpose had been buried in the rubble of war. My war torn heart had covered my reason for fighting.

> *It was necessary for me to achieve success and stability in order to answer the call.*

God showed me that it was necessary for me to engage systems in the marketplace that was necessary for me to gain the experiences of managing systems for navigating treacherous relationships and negotiating terms. It was necessary for me to achieve success and stability in order to answer the call. It was necessary because business changes you. Experiences inform you and security opens you up for risks. He said to me, "Now that you gained those things, now that the season of building and collecting is over, you became conflicted because it was time. So that season is over and it is time for you to return to your desire. You didn't lose it. It was covered and now it's time to recover it and to bury the guilt."

The desire to help resurfaced. My emotional and intellectual memory came flooding back, and slowly I had to reorganize my life. Things and people who were there out of the context of the desire to help had to be cutoff. Those who had latched on to what I had and not what had me was no longer accommodated in this season and God shifted me. The means is prosperity; the end is blessing, empowering, and helping others. The means justified the end, but only if you get back to the end.

Ultimate life fulfillment is growth and contribution to others. Fulfillment comes from finding ways to serve beyond ourselves.

Chapter 7

It Takes Courage to Lead

LEADERS, **PERFORM WITH EXCELLENCE.** So many people are waiting for the high position to operate in excellence. Excellence is a habit that must be practiced and cultivated. It does not come on you when you want it. It is practice that must be done daily until it becomes automatic. In the Bible, Paul prays for our love to abound more and more in knowledge and all discernment, so we may know what is excellent. As our love grows through our knowledge of Jesus' sacrifice and as we increase in our understanding of God's great plan for us, we should be strengthened in approaching all of our daily tasks with excellence. It becomes of no consequence what our task is or how remote.

If you can only preach in jail, give your best sermon. If you are preaching at the old folks' home, preach like they have 100 years ahead of them. If it's to one person, do it well. Take every opportunity and do it well. If you can't work well in obscurity, how can you be ready to be a celebrity? Do what you have to do well. Operate and serve where you are; it's not your destination. If you are at the "Mcjob," do that job as if you are the CEO. Show how you would want your employees to act. Save the company money as if it was yours.

Fry the hamburgers as if you were the customer with all the disposable cash. What are you doing? You are preparing for greatness. This is similar to being in a University and you are preparing to pass the test. It is your life. If it ended today, be able to say, I lived my life well. Jesus was a carpenter's son. He learned about wood and nail as well as humility and submission. He became prepared to die on a piece of wood with nails in His body and He did not say a word in defense of Himself. For 33 years before He began His public ministry, He was being prepared in obscurity. He was learning to master His flesh that His spirit would be prepared to offer His body as a living sacrifice. He was being prepared to do God's will and to fulfill God's purpose when He was elevated into the spotlight.

While you know that your obscurity is for a season, therefore, you can do good to others and be ready for your elevated success.

LEADERS Don't Major on the Minor: When I graduated from college, I graduated with a Bachelor's Degree. My major was journalism and my minor was social responsibility. I had to take most of my coursework in journalism in order to qualify for a Journalism degree. Even without a minor, I would meet the requirements for the degree in Journalism. Had I focused on the minor, I would not have qualified for a Journalism degree. I wouldn't even qualify for a degree period because a social responsibility degree was not offered as a major. In the same manner, we should not spend more time focusing on the details and less on the big picture.

I can't tell you the countless number of people I meet that are all into the detail and planning, and cannot get *any* business off the ground. They know where everything should go and how it should be. They plan and wait for everything to be just right and they plan and plan. The Bible says if we wait for the wind and the rain, we will not sow. God is in the details, but there is no perfect time, circumstance and situation unless you make it so. Step out even if it's not all perfect and pay attention to the big ideas – the major tasks.

I have met people who tell me they can't start because they don't know what part of town to start in or who to ask or what day of the week or what color. I recognize this as paralysis caused by a certain fear of loss expressed as, "I'm waiting for everything to line up or to know every detail." I tell these individuals, you are too bogged down in the details.

The website isn't ready, so I can't give out my business cards. I don't have cards, so I can't start the business. They have to get the cards right, the website right, and the marketing strategy right. Listen, what I have learned is that some details get worked out when the major components are engaged. Don't major on the minor, but seek to do what you are called to. Most people who start businesses don't know how the details will work out. They often don't know where the money will come from. They don't know where the partners are, or where the building will come from. They don't even know that much about social media. But they know that God called them to start that ministry or business, and they begin to do what that business or ministry is called to do. And as they continue, there is a response that happens and things come into focus, whereby time is given for the minor things to be aligned. It's just like wanting to buy your dream home, and after waiting for awhile, the opportunity presents itself and it is being sold at an affordable price. However, you won't buy it because you can't figure out what color you wanted to paint your child's bathroom. Majoring in the minor will often leave you without enough to do what God has called you to do.

This is even true in our attending to daily tasks. If we attended to the major tasks first everyday, we will be left with most of the day for the minor. But because we do both major and minor mixed together, we take all day and still have most things incomplete after a full day of work. Rather than doing the "must dos" first, we talk on the phone, answer unimportant emails, get more coffee, socialize at the water cooler, run errands and check on our favorite website. We even go on Facebook to see the latest post and post our pictures and messages. If instead, we would complete our "must dos" first, we will get more done. Therefore, the major items would be out of the way by midday and then you would be free to take part in all the minor things.

The majors are often avoided because it's hard work either emotionally or physically, but the hard tasks usually are important to your destiny.

I fight this battle by writing down all the "must dos" at the end of my work day for the next day. Then I go to my office and do all the "must dos" first, and on most days, I can finish the "must dos" by noon, if uninterrupted (which is unusual), however, I strive always to major on the major and not on the minor.

LEADERS THINK BIG: Leaders manage resources, set policies, and make decisions from the viewpoint of growth. How will your decisions now impact growth and how will it fit into a larger environment?

LEADERS GET THE RIGHT PEOPLE: Leaders get the right people in the right place. They identify the right people, inspire them, and then put them in the right place. Sometimes you have the right people, but they are performing tasks that they are not skilled or fulfilled in. You have to assess strengths and match strengths to task. It's easy when you are just starting or resource challenged to want to use people according to your need. Resist this temptation. The

Effective leaders focus not only on building a brand, but on building relationships.

wrong people or the right people in the wrong place will cause a monumental lack of productivity. Get the right people, put them in the right place, and let them go to work.

LEADERS ARE UP FRONT, BLUNT, AND CANDID: Leaders are upfront, nip it in the bud people. Let me define some of these words.

Blunt means call it out. Know for a surety, everybody already know the problem. Therefore, have everyone generate solutions. You want a leader who can take charge.

Candid means free from pretense or deceit. Say what you honestly feel. Be truthful. Everybody knows the liar in the room.

LEADERS DON'T BUILD A BRAND: Effective leaders focus is not only on building a brand, but on building relationships. Relationships built one at a time create a reputation. A reputation is what others say about you when you're not there or expect of you when you are there. My employees expect me to be no non-sense, fully informed, hopeful, and the hardest working person in the organization. When they go to others; they want to share. When they come to me; they want Godly counsel, viable solutions, and prayer. I have had many employees that I fired return to tell me how much they appreciate me. You can even build relationships by firing people timely, fairly and straightforwardly. Not firing people when needed can hurt your relationships and threaten your reputation.

Early on I thought that I was building relationship by giving employees many chances. I learned that employees who didn't appreciate me are those who saw me struggle with rehabilitating an employee rather than getting them "off the bus." The longer I put up with and gave chances to poor performing employees, the more credibility I lost both from the poor performing employee and the hard working ones.

LEADERS FORM PARTNERSHIPS: Whatever you can do on your own; you can do more if you partner with others. Two heads are better than one, iron does sharpen iron, and there is safety in a multitude of counsel. Without the partnership of my partners, I only would have my wisdom, my connections, and my resources to pull from. With them, I am three times as skilled, can be in three places at once, have three times the perspective, and have three people to hold me accountable. Partners are not full partners if they are only supporting you and your vision. In each of my partners, I encourage them to dream and pursue their vision. I lend my support and resources to them.

To sum up leaders' characteristics, think big, put the right people in the right place, be up front, be blunt and candid, don't build a brand, build relationships, and leverage the power of partnerships.

FINDING THE SACRED ASSIGNMENT: The big question is what is the sacred assignment and why are you not engaging in it? What are you doing with the image and likeness of God?

Every person is born with talents; equipped to meet the assignment with success. It's why Beethoven, Einstein, Martin Luther, Oprah Winfrey, Apostle Paul, Michael Angelo, Bill gates, Oral Roberts, and Barack Obama all became successful.

The almighty God, full of compassion through love gave us a gift called life and with it we have an opportunity to create, restore, impact, and make changes.

For me, my work is my reasonable act of worship. In the book of Luke, Chapter 13, the fig tree was cursed by Jesus because it had no fruit and without fruit it had no seed. Without seed it has no opportunity to multiply, increase or replenish the earth. If it had no purpose, then it had no assignment.

Luke 13:

> 6 Then he told this parable: "A man had a fig tree growing in his vineyard, and he went to look for fruit on it but did not find any.

> 7 So he said to the man who took care of the vineyard, 'For three years now, I've been coming to look for fruit on this fig tree and haven't found any. Cut it down! Why should it use up the soil?'

8 Sir, the man replied, 'leave it alone for one more year, and I'll dig around it and fertilize it.

9 If it bears fruit next year, fine! If not, then cut it down.

If we are enjoying the work of grace, and the privileges of the Holy Spirit, we must ask what is our purpose and pursue it with all our heart?

How would you like to prove God? How would you like to participate in God's story? God is calling you into your real life story.

As for me, I'm here to enforce the will of God on the earth, expand the kingdom of God, and to have His power dominating my sphere of influence. I identify with Christ. He and I are one. The Spirit of God lives in me. Therefore, I strive to only do what God says and speak only what God spoke or speaks. I am the "son of God" through Jesus Christ sent here to bless the earth and replenish it. I am created and called by God to be fruitful, to multiply, to increase and to live in abundance. I declare the return of the blessing and glory of God on the earth through Jesus

Christ's life, death, resurrection, and ascension. I am sent to bring the truth of the blessing as well as free the captives from bondage.

God is an awesome God, His power no foe can withstand. I have help continually available to me by God that I may establish His plan everywhere I go for He promised to be with me everywhere. Everything I need is already prepared and waiting for me. God wants me to do the extraordinary and to create a platform for His love to be revealed for the benefit of people all over the world. My economy are resources are in heaven. There is an unlimited supply given to me through Jesus Christ.

The plans for me are big and good. My gifts will make room for me and take me before kings. I will rebuild waste places and ruins. I will restore the breach. God is sending angels before me and I will release them to act on my behalf by speaking the Word of God.

THE IDYL

The latest enterprise in my life is the founding and development of a Charter School. The

Institute for the Development of Young Leaders (IDYL). It is a not for profit free school that was created to develop the whole child. It was created out of a sense of urgency to address the widening achievement gaps in education through including innovative approaches such as project based learning, service learning, family support services, and personal development coaching.

As we prepared to open our doors for the first time in 2013, we had a big vision and a small budget. Therefore, a percentage of all net proceeds of this book will go to the school's budget. Every book bought will be a seed planted in the life of a child. We have been plowing and pressing in to make this kingdom endeavor work, and God is constantly showing us His grace in the process. We are thankful to God that He has chosen us to do this, but we know the race is not given to the swift, but he that endureth to the end. We are in it to win it!

GENUINE WEALTH
I have spent a considerable amount of time talking about money, business, and wealth, and how it pertains to the acquisition of financial stability and

freedom. But wealth is not just about money. Wealth is about living well. It's about possessing a state of well-being. It is about being well in our personal, financial, spiritual, emotional, professional, and physical lives.

Genuine wealth is possessing the things that make life worthwhile. We are wealthy when we experience good relationships with our parents, siblings, spouses, and children. We are wealthy when we recognize opportunity in crisis, when we enjoy good health, when we live according to our callings. We are wealthy when we use our gifts and invest our talents to expand and add value to ourselves and others. We are wealthy when we have possession of the things that are valuable. Value means to have worth or be worthy. What has value in your life?

Value can facilitate the creation of social, personal, professional, spiritual, emotional and economic well-being. But too often rather than living our values, we seek to please others or to compromise as a way of acquiring the right position, or gaining the right person's favor. I've heard it said, if it's worth doing, it's worth doing well. Allow me to expand on this by saying, "If it's worth doing, do it to benefit others along with yourself." Don't do small. Do global. Genuine wealth is living a life worth living.

Live intending to *receive* the blessing, and to *release* the blessing.

INTENTION MATTERS

I want you to know a key ingredient to success is intention. Intention does matter. The motivation from which you launch your actions create pathways for the desire to be accomplished. The intention is the seed. If your intention or motivation is corrupt the fruit will be disaster. If your intention is pure to provide, protect or create then the fruit that it bears will be surprisingly delightful.

I am reminded of the great King Solomon. As it is written in 1 Kings, chapter 3, that the following night of the day that King Solomon was ordained King, he prayed and asked God for wisdom to lead the people. God's reply to King Solomon upon hearing his request, *"...because you did not ask for wealth or the death of your enemies but for a discerning heart so you may execute justice wisely, I will give you wisdom so great that there will never be anyone like you nor will there ever be. And I will give you what you have not asked for – both wealth and honor."* Because Solomon asked God for wisdom to rule over God's people wisely, he opened a door for wealth and honor.

His intention was to live a purpose filled life. A life lived to accomplish his tasks, using his position to bless others. His desire to carry out his responsibilities with great excellence, and his intention and commitment to live according to the purpose caused increase.

SACRIFICE

I would do you a disservice if I retold that great story of King Solomon's prayer and withheld an important truth. If you recall, I said that God told King Solomon to ask for whatever he wanted. Why would God say this? The scriptures reveal that after the kingdom was established in Solomon's hands, Solomon went to Gibeon, a city famous for an allegiance its inhabitants made with Joshua in order to prosper. And it was in this city that Solomon sacrificed 1000 bulls to God. Now you may not have 1000 bulls or $1000 dollars (if you do give it as an offering to your local church or to whom God speaks to you about); the point I am making here is a sacrifice is necessary to live intentionally for God's purpose in you to be fulfilled in your generation.

Increase requires sacrifice. In 2013 when I opened the charter school, I worked long and hard hours to open it. The days ran into nights and with a short nap, I was back in the saddle working in excess of 12 hour days while attempting to keep up with my other business enterprises. I was exhausted, lonely, missing my alone times, missing my hair and nail and luxury times. I was running hard wearing many hats, moving in a thousand directions. Then I received a note from a friend who was a Pastor. I will never forget the words she wrote. She said, "Thank you for the sacrifice you are making as an offering for the rest of us." That sent chills down my spine. It resonated with me and brought clarity to what I was doing. I was giving an offering to the success of the school. A sacrifice was required; for the paving of any way comes with sacrifice.

Too many of us are busied looking to get paid, or to make money, or make a living rather than being purposeful and living a life of legacy building. Stop making a living. It's time to make a legacy. When you live in your God-given purpose and intend to bless others and fulfill your assignment, the worst that can happen is you live a life that is full. You live a life that is blessed. The full life God intended for you. You live in your destiny. It is said of King David that he served God's purpose in his generation. May that be said of all of us.

If you live in greatness, no matter how small the situation, if your intentions are pure, if your purpose is to bless others, you will be great and you will unlock the open door of prosperity and wealth.

As I close this book, I want to pray for you. I pray that God will give you the spirit of wisdom and revelation in the knowledge of Him, and that He will open the eyes of your understanding that you might know exactly what He has called you to do. And that you may discern the riches of the glory of His inheritance for you and what is the exceeding greatness of His power toward you as you believe according to His power working in us.

May you understand the incomprehensible extravagance of His work in you, and that you may rise up now with endless energy and boundless strength!

And finally, may the Lord bless you and keep you, and make His face to shine upon you. May He lift up His countenance upon you and give you peace.

Made in the USA
Charleston, SC
11 April 2016